EDUCATION
TRAINING
YOUTH

# Integrating all young people into society through education and training

## Volume 2
## Compendium of the projects

EUROPEAN
COMMISSION

A great deal of additional information on the European Union is available on the Internet.
It can be accessed through the Europa server (http://europa.eu.int).

Cataloguing data can be found at the end of this publication.

Luxembourg: Office for Official Publications of the European Communities, 2000

Volume II: ISBN 92-828-7634-9
Volume I and II: ISBN 92-828-7630-6

Printed in Italy

PRINTED ON WHITE CHLORINE-FREE PAPER

# Table of contents

# Austria

## I. Brief description of the action

### 1.1. Name of the project
*Qualifizierter Helfer* (Qualified helper).

### 1.2. Organisation undertaking the action
AMS (*Arbeitsmarktservice*), BFI (*Berufsförderungsinstitut*), *Land Oberösterreich*, Project 'Countdown', Project magma (only for young females).

### 1.3. Address
Berufsschule Linz 7, Ferihumerstraße 28, A-4040 Linz.
City: Linz. Country: Austria.
Tel.: (43-732/733 036). Fax: (43-732/7330 36-18).
Contact Alois Reischl.

### 1.4. Brief description of the action
Young people selected out of 800 who did not succeed in getting a job (in Upper Austria), do get the chance to work at firms for three to four days per week and to go to school for one day. The firms do not have to pay any salary to these young people. The content of education is similar to that at vocational school (first year).

## II. Approach and content

### 2.1. Context, motivation and origin of the initiative
To help young people who did not succeed in getting a job, to get work and education.

### 2.2. Target group
The young people of the project 'Qualified helpers' are selected out of the group of those who did not succeed in getting a job at once, but want to work. Above all they also want to have an education. They are 15 to 16 years old.

### 2.3. Socio-educational approach

### 2.4. Scheduling and length of the action
Maximum two years.

### 2.5. Is your action/project in any way part of/supported by a national scheme or legislation that aims to combat social exclusion?
Supported by the Ministry of Education and in Upper Austria by the government.

## III. Partnerships and means used

**3.1. Name, status and role of the main partner**
Look at 1.2 and 2.5; also at the vocational school and selected firms.

**3.2. Other partners**

**3.3. Monitoring and ongoing evaluation**
The best evaluation of this help-system is to get a normal job for the young people after this training, especially in one of their favourite jobs.

**3.4. External evaluation of the action**
At vocational school they have tests and other examinations.

## IV. Resources

**4.1. Human resources used**
Teachers at vocational school and special guardians for work.

**4.2. Organisational and technical means used**
For the instructions at school the organisational and technical means of the commercial school they attend are used.

**4.3. Financial data**
Estimate of the cost of the action: ATS 300 000.

## V. Innovative features of the action

The young people can change during their education at any time to the 'dual system' if they get a job as an apprentice and they do not waste time.

## VI. Comments

Any support for young people to get a job and education is worthwhile. Any money invested in youth is great value.

# Belgium

## I. Brief description of the action

### 1.1. Name of the project

FAC Centre (centre providing combined training/work experience in construction). Operating in the various districts of Brussels Region, the Centre provides training in the construction trade for young people with few or no educational qualifications.

### 1.2. Organisation undertaking the action

The FAC Centre was set up in 1990 as a non-profit-making association by the various networks in Brussels Region dealing with State and private education. Its purpose is to work together with the CEFAs (combined training/work experience centres) to provide young people with few or no educational qualifications with the training they need to find jobs in the construction sector. Its aims have been extended as new needs have become apparent, and it now also provides training for unemployed adults and even goes into companies to train existing staff to act as mentors for the young people on training placements there.

The FAC Centre's Board of Governors is made up of the Directors of the three Brussels CEFAs.

### 1.3. Address

Address of the appointed representative:

Founder Member of the Centre and the Member of the General Assembly:

Loodts Jean, Boulevard Reyers, 45 Bte 6, 1030 Brussels.

Telephone and Fax: (32 (0)2) 735 88 45.

E-mail st001848@glo.be

Address of the FAC centre:

Rue de la Poste, 262

1030 Brussels

Tel. (32-2) 45 21 77.

Fax: (32-2) 41 01 32.

### 1.4. Brief description of the action

The Centre sets up close links with firms in the construction sector, which are asked to take on young people on training placements or on work contracts on a trial basis. The system is broadly as follows: basic training in the chosen trade in a semi-school setting (for young people aged under 18), training placement in a firm within the region, close monitoring of the various stages of training ensured by the Centre's close links with the firms involved. The Centre then keeps in touch with the trainees to help them find a stable job in one of the construction trades, and checks the conditions of any contract signed.

## II. Approach and content

### 2.1. Context, motivation and origin of the initiative

The principle of not overburdening companies with requests for help from various educational sectors dealing with training and monitoring young people with few or no educational qualifications was behind this move to coordinate the bodies concerned and channel their efforts into a specific production sector – in this case construction. The step was prompted by a desire for genuinely effective action on the part of the networks concerned.

The CEFAs, which in Belgium are specifically responsible for the training of young people with few or no educational qualifications, therefore joined forces in setting up and running an organisation to provide specific training in the construction trades: bricklaying, roofing, formwork, tiling, paving, etc. This means that the Centre is specialised in its training provision and has specific expertise in certain trades. Its specialist status has been recognised by other training organisations, which have been able to take advantage of that expertise.

## 2.2. Target group

The main target group is young people in a situation of exclusion who have not completed compulsory schooling. These can be divided into three groups: the under-18s, the over-18s and the adult unemployed. The Centre follows the European recommendations in this area in seeking paid apprenticeship contracts or work contracts for its trainees.

## 2.3. Socio-educational approach

Most of the young people come from poor backgrounds, often in the socially excluded category (immigrants, for example). Their education tends to have been patchy and they have not been able to follow any kind of vocational course, being put off by even the very limited theoretical content dealing with the technical aspects of the trade.

The first step towards a successful outcome is to accustom the young person to a work routine in a way which will not remind him of school. This means concentrating on practicalities, which is the only approach young people in this situation will find acceptable. The training is, therefore, based on practical work techniques reproducing real-life working conditions, even in the Centre's workshops.

The trainers are specialised in the techniques of the trades concerned. Being former manual workers themselves, they talk the language of the trade and have the right kind of down-to-earth directness.

## 2.4. Scheduling and length of the action

We have had to re-think the traditional idea of progress by academic year; the training for these young people, who are organised into homogenous groups as far as possible, is paced according to progress and, obviously, to fit in with any placement, however temporary, offered by one of the firms supporting the programme.

## 2.5. Is your action/project in any way part of supported by a national scheme or legislation that aims to combat social exclusion?

The Belgian national programme subsidises training for young people dropping out of school via the training departments or CEFAs. The FAC Centre is largely dependent on these subsidies, which are scaled according to the number of people placed with us by each CEFA.

Other sources of assistance for essentials are:

Funds and equipment for the workshops, provided by the employers' association, regional chambers of the building trades, specific trade associations within the construction industry, etc.

— Subsidies to cover the remuneration of qualified staff for monitoring of the trainees progress (social workers, psychologists, etc.) from the European Social Fund (FORCE or ADAPT projects).

— Subsidies for staff for one-off training sessions organised in response to requests from ORBEM (employment promotion organisation) or from *Brussels Formation* and the COCOF (support plan for the unemployed).

— Premises for training workshops provided by the *Commune* of Schaerbeek.

# III.  Partnerships and means used

### 3.1.  Name, status and role of the main partner

The main partners are the three CEFA *'Ecoles'* (formerly the 'part-time education centres') in Brussels Region, which are approved and recognised by Belgium's French Community. These institutions have a dynamic Board of Governors that holds frequent meetings to organise the FAC's activities. The non-profit-making FAC association holds an annual general meeting, which is attended by the founder members as well as the governors. These partners are responsible for the budget, managing expenditure and recruitment of staff, and planning the Association's activities.

### 3.2.  Other partners

The principle behind the FAC association being to cast its net wider in the interests of more extensive and more effective training, it is keen to open its doors to any other potential partners. Its resources and experience are at the disposal of anyone who requires them. It has, for example, begun providing training for electricians, crane drivers, industrial labourers (tutoring), etc.

### 3.3.  Monitoring and ongoing evaluation

The Directors of the three CEFAs are very much aware of their responsibilities in respect of the running and management of the FAC. To this end they keep careful statistics on such aspects as the number of young people on apprenticeship training, the number of under-18s on the books, the number of training contracts signed, the number of trainers employed, accounts, etc.

### 3.4.  External evaluation of the action

Over the past nine years, the FAC has gained considerable experience in training young people in social difficulty and helping them to fulfil their potential. This experience is recognised by other partners working in this field, who are more than ready to work together with the Centre for effective results.


# IV.  Resources

### 4.1.  Human resources used

Estimated human resources employed on average since the creation of the FAC are around 20 persons working full-time.

### 4.2.  Organisational and technical means used

While keeping up to date with the developments in new technologies, the FAC Centre devotes most of its attention to the requirements of the jobs for which the young people and the unemployed are being trained. Examples are the new formwork construction methods, reading of plans, etc.

### 4.3.  Financial data

General

Given the large number of training sessions and the different partners involved, the FAC Centre calculates its staffing costs per teacher/hour per year and per head/trainee.

This varies between BEF 180 and BEF 255, depending on the group concerned (staffing and administrative costs, equipment, etc.).

Broken down by financial and technical and human resources:

— Investment: a certain capitalisation is necessary to provide for the variation in the training workload. The Board of Governors does not consider this capital excessive.

— Running costs: a significant feature of the Centre's organisation is that its staffing needs vary with the training requirements. This type of organisation obviously imposes certain constraints in terms of constant restructuring of the training teams, ongoing evaluation of performance, problems vis-à-vis their qualifications, etc.

## V.    Innovative features of the action

We believe that these lie essentially in the following:

— Association of training institutions in order to explore jointly a specific sphere of industry in a given region with a view to being accepted as having a right of representation within that sphere.
— Concentration of practical training methods in closely-related fields to ensure mastery of even the most technical aspects and to ensure that the training specifications are geared as realistically as possible to the possibilities of the target group (in terms of manual skills, technical aptitude, practical intelligence).
— Acceptance of what is essentially a coordinating role, in this specific field, for various training and role-specification schemes.

## VI.    Comments

A total of 1 200 persons have passed through our training schemes over the past eight years, representing an average of around 150 young people and adults per year. The success rate (based on whether the trainee is still in a job within the same field one year after training) is between 60 and 75 % for young people and 90 % for the unemployed.

# I. Brief description of the action

### 1.1. Name of the project
Neighbourhood Contract.

### 1.2. Organisation undertaking the action
Commune of Ixelles and Brussels-Capital Region.

### 1.3. Address
Hotel. Communal, chaussée d'Ixelles; 168-1050 Brussels.
City: Brussels. Country: Belgium.
Phone and Fax: (32-2) 512 96 75.
Contact: Rachid Madrane.

### 1.4. Brief description of the action
Neighbourhood urban regeneration programme.
Various measures: Socio-occupational integration; urban renewal of the residential environment and public areas; integrated approach involving the participation of all those playing an active role at local level.

# II. Approach and content

### 2.1. Context, motivation and origin of the initiative

### 2.2. Target group
Urban renewal: all inhabitants of the district; socio-occupational integration: *idem*.

### 2.3. Socio-educational approach
Concept of integrated development at local level.

### 2.4. Scheduling and length of the action
Four years.

### 2.5. Is your action/project in any way supported by a national scheme or legislation that aims to combat social exclusion?
Yes: *Fonds d'Impulsion* policy towards immigrants, living in harmony with each other, integration, aid for urban renewal (URBAN not selected).

# III. Partnerships and means used

### 3.1. Name, status and role of the main partner
The commune, region, local associations, inhabitants of the district.

### 3.2. Other partners

### 3.3. Monitoring and ongoing evaluation

### 3.4. External evaluation of the action

# IV. Resources

### 4.1. Human resources used
1. General coordinator of the neighbourhood contract.
2. Neighbourhood mediator.

**4.2.** **Organisational and technical means used**
Creation of an information centre.
Local office for employment and training.

**4.3.** **Financial data**
Estimate of the cost of the action:
* overall: ± BEF 300 400 000 over four years;
* when distinguishing various financial contributions and making available of technical
* and human means
 — in investment terms: 90 %
 — in operating costs: 10 %.

## V. Innovative features of the action
Integrated development in cooperation with the inhabitants.

## VI. Comments

# I. Brief description of the action

### 1.1. Name of the project
EDIT Asbl (*Equipe d'insertion dans le travail*).

### 1.2. Organisation undertaking the action
*Idem.*

### 1.3. Address
Boulevard Piercot 31B.
City: Liège - 4000. Country: Belgium.
Tel: (32-4) 222 41 41. Fax: *Idem.*
Contact: Mme Grisay.

### 1.4. Brief description of the action:
Social and occupational integration of low-skilled job seekers. Consolidation of foundation skills alternating with periods of in-company training.

# II. Approach and content

### 2.1. Context, motivation and origin of the initiative
Objective: to get at least 60 % of participants into jobs or further vocational training by the end of the training period.

### 2.2. Target group
Low-skilled job seekers (at most, they have completed fourth year secondary technical school).
Mixed population group of 18 to 30-year olds.

### 2.3. Socio-educational approach
Preparation and implementation of customised training plan.
Close partnership with SMEs in the Liège region.

### 2.4. Scheduling and length of the action
Six-month module for 20 participants, alternating between consolidation of foundation skills, theory and periods of in-company training.

### 2.5. Is your action/project in any way part of supported by a national scheme or legislation that aims to combat social exclusion?
EDIT receives ESF aid under Objective 3, measure 1.1 and 2.1, and is a signatory to the Charter on Pathways to Integration organised by the Walloon regional authorities.

# III. Partnerships and means used

### 3.1. Name, status and role of the main partner
Companies in the region: taking in trainees, providing them with practical training, and recruiting them at the end of the training period.

### 3.2. Other partners
FOREM: Art. 6 of the relevant agreement.
*Promotion Sociale*: involvement in the training.

### 3.3. Monitoring and ongoing evaluation
Monthly progress reports on the trainees.
'Log' book.

Trainees' assessment of the training.
Evaluation of the module.

   **3.4.**    **External evaluation of the action**
FOREM supervision (in accordance with Art. 6 of the relevant agreement).

## IV.   Resources

   **4.1.**    **Human resources used**
Liège: 4 (women) trainers: 1 coordinator + 3 university-trained + external trainers.
Verviers: 3 (women) trainers + external trainers.

   **4.2.**    **Organisational and technical means used**
Training software.
Cameras + TV.

   **4.3.**    **Financial data**

## V.   Innovative features of the action
Specific approach to the training situation.

## VI.   Comments

# I. Brief description of the action

### 1.1. Name of the project
'Simply a school'.

### 1.2. Organisation undertaking the action
Maison des associations ASBL.

### 1.3. Address
City: Brussels. Country: Belgium.
Tel.: (32-2) 514 18 80. Fax: (32-2) 514 00 66.
E-mail: simplementecole@infonie.be
Contact: Maurice Corneal.

### 1.4. Brief description of the action:
Project aimed at re-socialising truant schoolchildren and young people who have dropped out of training in order to get them back into training leading to a qualification on the basis of a personal project.

# II. Approach and content

### 2.1. Context motivation and origin of the initiative
Providing a response to the problem of truancy among young people from a socially brittle district.

### 2.2. Target group
Young people aged 10 to 18 or more having dropped out of traditional school/training.

### 2.3. Socio-educational approach
Active and participative teaching approaches, individual monitoring of the student's overall problems, in-company training period.

### 2.4. Scheduling and length of the action
The action will go on throughout the school year.

### 2.5. Is your action/project in any way part of/supported by a national scheme or legislation that aims to combat social exclusion?
Action supported by the French-speaking Community and the European Commission (DG XXII).

# III. Partnerships and means used

### 3.1. Name, status and role of the main partner
Ultimately, to reintegrate these young people in the schools of the Brussels 'zone', i.e. a group of 25 schools of the French-speaking community.

### 3.2. Other partners
Juvenile justice departments, and three similar European projects being undertaken in France and Scotland.

### 3.3. Monitoring and ongoing evaluation

### 3.4. External evaluation of the action

## IV.    Resources

### 4.1.    Human resources used
Two teachers working on a half-time basis; one social worker (full time); one psychologist (half-time).

### 4.2.    Organisational and technical means used
Reception structure, use of computer-based resources (CD-ROM, Web, etc.).

### 4.3.    Financial data
Estimate of the cost of the action:
- overall: ECU 90 000 yearly;

## V.    Innovative features of the action
Unique and innovatory action in French-speaking Belgium.

## VI.    Comments

# I.    Brief description of the action

### 1.1.    Name of the project
'Second chance school'.

### 1.2.    Organisation undertaking the action
*Centre d'éducation et de formation en alternance- CEFA — de Saint Gilles.*

### 1.3.    Address
Rue de la Croix de Pierre 73.
City: 1060 Saint Giles. Country: Belgium.
Tel: (32-2) 537 55 37. Fax: (32-2) 537 55 37.
Contact: Marie-Jo Sanchez.

### 1.4.    Brief description of the action
This social and occupational integration project targets two age groups: the 15- to 18-year-olds and the 18- to 25-year-olds, with an obligation for the first to attend school on a part-time basis. The aim is to organise sandwich training for the overall target population of 15- to 25-year-olds, opening on to occupational integration in partnership with business and industry.

# II.    Approach and content

### 2.1.    Context, motivation and origin of the initiative
Dovetailing teaching approaches and statutory arrangements situated at various tiers of administration in Belgium.

### 2.2.    Target group
Young people aged 15 to 25 having dropped out of school and without any sort of vocational qualification.

### 2.3.    Socio-educational approach
The approach addresses the specific features of the problem in Belgium and seeks to combine the need to stem truancy with an endeavour to implement sandwich-type vocational training.

### 2.4.    Scheduling and length of the action
The project must blend into the regional context.

### 2.5.    Is your action/project in any way part of/supported by a national scheme or legislation that aims to combat social exclusion?
Recognition by the Brussels regional authorities and by the Ministry of Education as a player in social and occupational integration.
ESF.

# III.    Partnerships and means used

### 3.1.    Name, status and role of the main partner
The Saint Gilles CEFA is an educational establishment involved in qualification and certification, and is also a player in social and occupational integration.

### 3.2.    Other partners
Counselling and support centres, plus non-profit organisations active in local integration schemes.

**3.3. Monitoring and ongoing evaluation**

The project would be undertaken in conjunction with players from the business sector, the world of training and from the public authorities concerned.

**3.4. External evaluation of the action**

Mainly by the public authorities providing subsidies.

## IV. Resources

**4.1. Human resources used**

**4.2. Organisational and technical means used**

School facilities in general and open access to multimedia resources.

**4.3. Financial data**

## V. Innovative features of the action

It would be the first structure which caters for all the priorities and criteria of social and occupational integration policies.

## VI. Comments

# Denmark

## I. Brief description of the action

### 1.1. Name of the project
TAMU-Training Centre for Young People.

### 1.2. Organisation undertaking the action
AMU-Labour Market Training System (Ministry of Employment).

### 1.3. Address
TAMU — Viborggade 70, 2100 Copenhagen, Denmark.
City: Copenhagen. Country: Denmark.
Tel.: (45) 35 25 03 40. Fax: (45) 35 25 03 55.
Contact: Lars Kramer Mikkelsen.

### 1.4. Brief description of the action
In the course period participants will be introduced to practical work and production combined with theoretical teaching and the purpose is to provide participants with skills and social competence which can form the basis for ensuring a job or continuing education.

## II. Approach and content

### 2.1. Context, motivation and origin of the initiative
The origin of the initiative is the consequence-oriented practice, in which the individual participant learns to understand to take concrete responsibility for own actions.

### 2.2. Target group
TAMU is especially aimed at young people aged 18 to 30, available for work but unable to obtain any other education. TAMU is an offer to the weakest group in the labour market.

### 2.3. Socio-educational approach
Because of no realistic opportunities of obtaining qualifying training under any other legislation, TAMU takes care of specific personal and social problems.

### 2.4. Scheduling and length of the action
The total duration of the training programme is 30 weeks. In case of absence the programme will be extended automatically. The normal duration is 40 to 42 weeks.

### 2.5. Is your action/project in any way part of/supported by a national scheme or legislation that aims to combat social exclusion?
TAMU is part of a national legislation with the special aim to constitute the weakest group with personal and social problems.

## III. Partnerships and means used

**3.1.** Name, status and role of the main partner

**3.2.** Other partners

**3.3.** Monitoring and ongoing evaluation

**3.4.** External evaluation of the action

## IV. Resources

**4.1. Human resources used**
One teacher (technical and personal) for 8 to 12 participants.
TAMU has five centres in Denmark with 250 to 300 participants. The through flow will be 400 to 600 per year.

**4.2. Organisational and technical means used**
The facilities are based on the different workplaces and technical, vocational areas.

**4.3. Financial data**
Estimate of the cost of the action:
Around USD 7 million taken from the national labour market training programme.

## V. Innovative features of the action

## VI. Comments

# I.   Brief description of the action

### 1.1.   Name of the project
The whole orientated effort towards people threatened by lifelong marginalisation.

### 1.2.   Organisation undertaking the action
*Ella and Moller Sorigs Fond.*

### 1.3.   Address
Hovedgaden 52.
City: 9480 Lokken. Country: Denmark.
Tel: (45) 98 88 30 10. Fax: (45) 98 88 30 10.
E-mail: dhi-soerig@nethotel.dk
Contact: Ojvind Ottensen.

### 1.4.   Brief description of the action
The whole orientated effort is a purposeful offer, aiming to give the individual a sense and experience of connection and whole in the living of life. Due to this, a realistic scheme is initiated in collaboration with the 'support and contact' arrangement.

# II.   Approach and content

### 2.1.   Context, motivation and origin of the initiative

### 2.2.   Target group
Young people aged from 24 years with special needs and qualifications, most of them receive a social pension.

### 2.3.   Socio-educational approach

### 2.4.   Scheduling and length of the action
This action goes for four years (1996 to 1999).

### 2.5.   Is your action/project in any way part of/supported by a national scheme or legislation that aims to combat social exclusion?
*Ella & Moller Sorigs Fond* is a private organisation, which is supported by national legislation and the local authority.

# III.   Partnerships and means used

### 3.1.   Name, status and role of the main partner
We have partnership with the local authorities, which pays for our supporting of young people.

### 3.2.   Other partners

### 3.3.   Monitoring and ongoing evaluation

### 3.4.   External evaluation of the action

# IV.   Resources

### 4.1.   Human resources used
Our teachers and social workers have experience in the occupation being taught.

# I. Brief description of the action

### 1.1. Name of the project
*Projekt skolen Grennessminde i Tåstrup.*

### 1.2. Organisation undertaking the action
*Grennessminde i Tåstrup.*

### 1.3. Address
Køgevej 175.
City: 2630 Tåstrup. Country: Denmark.
Phone: (45) 43 99 04 70. Fax: (45) 43 52 04 70.
Contact: Eva Graff.

### 1.4. Brief description of the action:
Job and residential training for about 90 young slow-learning pupils aged 17 to 25.
Eleven practical workshops with production of goods sold to private clients and firms, one workshop with social training, agreement with firms about vocational training of the pupils.
We also use the established special schools to teach the pupils in Danish, Maths and data.

# II. Approach and content

### 2.1. Context, motivation and origin of the initiative
A group of parents started the project in 1984 with six pupils and the project has slowly developed since. The project was started because there were no offers to this target group earlier.

### 2.2. Target group
Slow-learning young persons aged 17 to 25.

### 2.3. Socio-educational approach
Social training of the pupils, learning how to manage both in living and getting and keeping a job.
Our target group has to learn how to behave socially to be accepted by other people and to learn how to manage in living alone, cooking, cleaning, paying the rent and so on.

### 2.4. Scheduling and length of the action
The action lasts as long as the pupil needs training, on average, two to three years.

### 2.5. Is your action/project in any way part of/supported by a national scheme or legislation which aims to combat social exclusion
We are part of a project supported by the Social Ministry, called DHI, but otherwise the project is an independent institution.

# III. Partnerships and means used

### 3.1. Name, status and role of the main partner
We cooperate mainly with communities all over Denmark

### 3.2. Other partners
Schools, firms.

### 3.3. Monitoring and ongoing evaluation
We evaluate the project intern continually.

### 3.4. External evaluation of the action

## IV.    Resources

### 4.1.    Human resources used
Some 32 teachers, administrative personal, workmen.

### 4.2.    Organisational and technical means used

### 4.3.    Financial data

## V.    Innovative features of the action

## VI.    Comments

# I. Brief description of the action

### 1.1. Name of the project
*DHI (Den helhedsorienterde Indsats).*

### 1.2. Organisation undertaking the action
*Produktionshojskolen i Svendborg.*

### 1.3. Address
Hellegardsvej 63, 5700.
City: Svendborg. Country: Denmark.
Tel.: (45) 62 22 41 10. Fax: (45) 62 22 81 14.
E-mail: phs@pbs.dk
Contact: Peter Guldstadt.

### 1.4. Brief description of the action
A presentation of a production in a high school in Denmark. The school has a special programme for young people who need special support in trying to make a personal future.

# II. Approach and content

### 2.1. Context, motivation and origin of the initiative
The school is a place where production, instruction and general life skills are integrated into a whole: A school about life and a school for life.

### 2.2. Target group
A school for young people who cannot take part in ordinary education without help. Their ages are from 16 to 25 years. Both men and women.

### 2.3. Socio-educational approach
A special teacher takes care of the students' free time. Where to stay, help them to be independent of social support.

### 2.4. Scheduling and length of the action
A person can start at any time of the year — provided there are places vacant. They can stay at the school until we, together with the young person, have found what to do.

### 2.5. Is your action/project in any way part of/supported by a national scheme or legislation that aims to combat social exclusion?
We have some support. During DHI the Danish Government pays the special teachers. The Danish Government pays us for teaching from 8 to 3 p.m. daily.

# III. Partnerships and means used

### 3.1. Name, status and role of the main partner
DHI.

### 3.2. Other partners
The schools who are connected to DHI.

### 3.3. Monitoring and ongoing evaluation
During the DHI project.

### 3.4. External evaluation of the action
*Idem.*

## IV.     Resources

### 4.1.     Human resources used
This is complicated.  Cannot be described in four lines.

### 4.2.     Organisational and technical means used

### 4.3.     Financial data

## V.     Innovative features of the action
Will be described during DHI project.

## VI.     Comments

# I. Brief description of the action

### 1.1. Name of the project
Blue College.

### 1.2. Organisation undertaking the action
Blue Cross, Denmark.

### 1.3. Address
Sdr. Hedevej 7.
City: 6623 Vorbasse. Country: Denmark.
Tel: (45) 75 33 35 04. Fax: (45) 75 33 35 85.
Contact: Peter Guldstadt.

### 1.4. Brief description of the action:
Integration into society and education and training with a view to gain employment.


# II. Approach and content

### 2.1. Context, motivation and origin of the initiative
The project is the Danish Second Chance pilot project initiated by Blue Cross Denmark — an alcohol abuse-combating organisation.

### 2.2. Target group
Marginalised youths 18 to 25 years of age, excluded from education and unable to gain access to employment.

### 2.3. Socio-educational approach
A whole oriented approach containing education, skill development, and social training and personal empowerment

### 2.4. Scheduling and length of the action

### 2.5. Is your action/project in any way part of/supported by a national scheme or legislation that aims to combat social exclusion?
Blue College in the Danish Second Chance School pilot project.


# III. Partnerships and means used

### 3.1. Name, status and role of the main partner
(a) Ribe County is political base.
(b) Danish Education Ministry technical and political partner.

### 3.2. Other partners
Blue Cross Denmark is responsible for implementation and owner of the project.

### 3.3. Monitoring and ongoing evaluation

### 3.4. External evaluation of the action
Danish Teachers' Academy.

## IV.    Resources

**4.1.    Human resources used**
New staff is being recruited.

**4.2.    Organisational and technical means used**

**4.3.    Financial data**
Estimate of the cost of the action: DKK 3.5 million  = about ECU 450 000 p.a.

## V.    Innovative features of the action

1.  Three components in one: training of marginalised youths, training of resourceful youths (volunteers), exchange with other similar projects.
2.  Capacity to deal with alcohol and drug abuse.
3.  Church affiliation giving a base of Christian values.

## VI.    Comments

The project is only just restarting after having been reorganised thoroughly.  New project head has just been appointed and will join on 1 May 1998.

# I.  Brief description of the action

### 1.1.  Name of the project
DHI/PAU.

### 1.2.  Organisation undertaking the action
Vejle kommune.
Vejle kommunale ungdomsskole.

### 1.3.  Address
Enghavevej 34.
City: 7100 Vejle. Country: Denmark.
Tel.: (45) 75 72 72 99. Fax: (45) 75 72 71 99.
Contact: Eva Søndergaard.

### 1.4.  Brief description of the action:
PAU: Practical common education for slow learners. Focus is laid on establishing life quality through resident training, employment training and education.


# II.  Approach and content

### 2.1.  Context, motivation and origin of the initiative
Origin: to prevent marginalisation.
Motivation: to avoid young people sliding out of the labour market and our education systems.
Context: as in 1.4.

### 2.2.  Target group
A person who has not been able to use what education and employment has to offer.
Age: 16 to 25.

### 2.3.  Socio-educational approach
Empowerment.

### 2.4.  Scheduling and length of the action
FUU: 2 years (3).
EGU: 2 years (3).
PAU: 3 years.
Bridge building: 3 years.

### 2.5.  Is your action/project in any way part of/supported by a national scheme or legislation that aims to combat social exclusion?
Partly Government legislation (FUU-EGU).
Government financed.


# III.  Partnerships and means used

### 3.1.  Name, status and role of the main partner
DHI 'the Whole Orientated Effort'.
A project under the Social Ministry and the Vejle Kommune.

### 3.2.  Other partners
Five DHI projects in Denmark.

**3.3.    Monitoring and ongoing evaluation**
Management group.

**3.4.    External evaluation of the action**
Ålborg University.


## IV.    Resources

**4.1.    Human resources used**
FUU: 1 teacher.
EGU: 0 teacher.
Bridge building: 6 teachers.
PAU: 4 teachers.

**4.2.    Organisational and technical means used**
Electronic data processing. Internet. Intranet.

**4.3.    Financial data**
Estimate of the cost of the action:
Overall, DKK 3 800 000.
When distinguishing various financial contributions and making available of technical and human means:
— in investment terms
— in operating costs.
Salaries: teachers: 80 %.
Equipment, hardware: 20 %.


## V.    Innovative features of the action
Whole orientated effort into the projects:
PAU
FUU
EGU
Bridge building class.


## VI.    Comments

# Finland

## I. Brief description of the action

### 1.1. Name of the project
My Own Career.

### 1.2. Organisation undertaking the action
My Own Career Association, Finland.

### 1.3. Address
City: Kuopio. Country: Finland.
Tel: (358-50) 569 11 66. Fax: (358-17) 18 44 60.
E-mail: jukka.onttonen@tekeva.pp.fi
Contact: Jukka Onttonen.

### 1.4. Brief description of the action
Providing education and training using a productive learning approach, integrating youth through real working life.

To build up a network of local alternative projects in Finland, using and developing the own-career methods.

Open the schools to society (city as school) and help cross-professional teams work together to avoid exclusion.

## II. Approach and content

### 2.1. Context, motivation and origin of the initiative
Within the school context desire to use new teaching methods to avoid social exclusion and to improve school motivation and to develop models in four different levels: individual, local, national and international. The Own Career project offers a possibility for a youngster to whom the traditional way of school is not suitable and produces exclusion.

### 2.2. Target group
9th/10th grade pupils (14- to 18-years-old) with high school failure and high risk of exclusion in different levels.

### 2.3. Socio-educational approach
Learning by doing — developing social abilities through adventure camps (experiences in nature), discussion session, tutoring and training. Individual curriculum, holistic approach. Influencing social environment of the youngsters by experience-education and individual planning.

### 2.4. Scheduling and length of the action
Two new Own Career groups (or more) every year. Research-project from year 1998.

Enlarging the actions into new target groups as vocational education (alternative) and young immigrants in 1999 at latest. Every local project should become part of every-day education in five years.

**2.5.** **Is your action/project in any way part of/supported by a national scheme or legislation that aims to combat social exclusion?**
Our action is part of educational system with alternative approach, parallel with normal educational system.

## III. Partnerships and means used

**3.1.** **Name, status and role of the main partner**
Local communities and administration, enterprises, associations available in different cities, Ministry of Education.

**3.2.** **Other partners**
Different schools.
Different projects at international level, for example INEPS.

**3.3.** **Monitoring and ongoing evaluation**
Individual evaluation periodically, self-evaluation and reporting, discussion results.
Follow-up study with Helsinki University of all Own Career youngsters.

**3.4.** **External evaluation of the action**
Helsinki University.
Smaller studies in other universities.
Evaluation meetings between different groups at local level.

## IV. Resources

**4.1.** **Human resources used**
Special education teacher/group.
Youth care workers/group.
Mentors in enterprises for every youngster.

**4.2.** **Organisational and technical means used**
Association, PCs.

**4.3.** **Financial data**

## V. Innovative features of the action

Multi-professional cooperation in the projects (teachers, youth-workers, police, etc.)
Experience-education (camps etc.).
Open school (city as school) produces learning outside the school walls.
Integration of the youth through learning and by taking responsibility of everyone's own choices.
To get an official model within the traditional school-system.

## VI. Comments

My Own Career Association is a facilitator of people and actions. The Association produces materials and helps local actions to fight for resources within very traditional school system. My Own Career is the first project in Finland to develop new ways to fight against exclusion inside schools, not after.

# I.  Brief description

### 1.1.  Name of the project
Alternative Vocational Institute (*Vaihtoehtoinen Ammattikoulu*).

### 1.2.  Organisation undertaking the action
*Sovinto ry Suomen Setlementtisäätiö.*

### 1.3.  Address
Haukilahdenkatu 4.
FIN 00550 Helsinki, Finland.
Tel.: (358-9) 73 57 63. Fax: (358-9) 73 57 63.
Contact: Hannu AHTI.

### 1.4.  Brief description of the action
The institute organises vocational training in 10 sectors for young excluded people, often with a criminal background. The duration of the studies varies from 10 months up to two years.


# II.  Approach and content

### 2.1.  Content, motivation and origin of the initiative
The Alternative Vocational Institute was established in 1991, based on the experience gathered in the settlement proceedings of young criminals in order to avoid imprisonment and other jurisdictional sanctions. Since most of the youngsters were found to be school failures, the principle idea is to adapt the school to better address to the needs of the trainees. The training is integrated into the work: the school has a large number of clients and the trainees work with real cases, e.g. in repairing of crashed cars. The trainees form cooperatives to serve the clients.

### 2.2.  Target group
The Alternative Vocational Institute recruits young people of 17 to 24 years of age from prisons, reception centres, social welfare centres and from the local branches of *Kriminaalihuoltoyhdistys* (association for probation and aftercare of criminals). Some of the trainees are around 30 years of age in order to bring experience to the group. All trainees are long-term unemployed and more than 80 % are male.

### 2.3.  Socio-educational approach

### 2.4.  Scheduling and length of the action
The school has been running on a continuous basis since 1991, most of the recruits on a non-stop basis throughout the year.

### 2.5.  Is your action/project in any way part of or supported by a  national scheme or legislation which aims to combat social exclusion
No


# III.  Partnership and means used

### 3.1.  Name, status and role of the main partners
A group of 50  enterprises of motor vehicle import and car sales and catering form a group that use the services of the trainees and also employ them.

### 3.2.  Other partners

### 3.3. Monitoring and ongoing evaluation

The main financing bodies, i.e. the Labour Authority through the Employment and Economic Development Centres and the Educational Office of the City of Helsinki are informed about the proceedings on a continuous basis.

### 3.4. External evaluation of the action

The Helsinki College of Social Affairs carries out an evaluation and monitoring of the school on a continuous basis. This is not based on a demand of the financing bodies but on an interest to follow the progress and the results of the school.

## IV. Resources

### 4.1. Human resources

The school employs 10 teachers or workshop leaders. The personality of a teacher is the basis of teaching. So, the criteria for the selection of teachers are, in this order, (i) the personality, (ii) a long experience of the subject matter and (iii) formal qualifications.

### 4.2. Organisational and technical means used

Information technology is included in all curricula but is not a major means of teaching.

### 4.3. Financial data

Estimate of the cost of action: the annual budget is at the level of FIM 5.5 million which equals ECU 930 000. The funding for the school comes from (a) the Employment and Economic Development Centres and ESF Objective 3; (b) the Educational Office/City of Helsinki; (c) from the Ministry of Education; and (d) for the rehabilitation, from the Finnish Slot Machine Association.

## V. Innovative features of the action

The school has been running since 1991, so perhaps we should talk about what is different from other actions more than from what is innovative. The training is fully integrated into the work the trainees do for their clients. The approach is client oriented. The self-confidence and self-esteem are constructed while experiences of successfully finished operations with real cases are gathered. The school follows an approach entitled 'consequence pedagogy' where the trainees themselves carry full responsibility for their actions. Rehabilitation of the trainees plays also an important role.

## VI. Comments

The results of the Alternative Vocational Institute quite remarkable. According to an external evaluation 67 % of the trainees are employed in the labour market.

# I. Brief description of the action

### 1.1. Name of the project
Topspin-training opportunities for special needs integration  (Leonardo da Vinci programme).

### 1.2. Organisation undertaking the action
Helsinki Roihuvuori Vocational College.

### 1.3. Address
Prinsessantie 2 00820 Helsinki.
City: Helsinki.  Country: Finland.
Tel.: (358-9) 31 08 47 08. Fax: (358-9) -31 08 47 10.
E-mail: eeva.laurila@raol.edu.hel.fi
Contact: Laurila Eeva.

### 1.4. Brief description of the action
The project Topspin is designed to develop an assessment procedure with matching support strategies for students with moderate learning difficulties. The project creates a complete 'protection net' which systematically and objectively helps the student and spreads information between the teachers and other school staff.

# II. Approach and content

### 2.1. Context, motivation and origin of the initiative
Until now, there has not been a systematic way to find out students' needs, help them achieve their studies and in that way prevent exclusion. The system created in this Leonardo da Vinci project and used now for the students with moderate learning difficulties will be enlarged to concern every student in the pilot colleges.

### 2.2. Target group
Students with moderate learning difficulties in vocational training, aged from 16 to 20.

### 2.3. Socio-educational approach
To help the youngsters to get a diploma and find a job is most important for their future and an efficient way for preventing the exclusion

### 2.4. Scheduling and length of the action
Topspin is a three-year pilot project (1995-98). However, the system created in this project will be enlarged to the whole college, to form the basis of student welfare.

### 2.5. Is your action/project in any way part of/supported by a national scheme or legislation that aims to combat social exclusion?
This project creates equal opportunities for students with moderate learning difficulties to be able to find jobs by diagnosing their special needs at a very early level. This way the students do not drop out and can have extra support.

# III. Partnerships and means used

### 3.1. Name, status and role of the main partner
Mid-Kent College, England; ROC Zeeland, Holland; Enskede Gård Gymnasium, Sweden.

### 3.2. Other partners
Provincial State Office of Southern Finland; City of Helsinki, Youth Department; Mid-Kent Education Business.

**3.3.**   **Monitoring and ongoing evaluation**

Further education for educational staff, reflecting discussions and regular meetings in each project country regularly.

**3.4.**   **External evaluation of the action**

The project has an evaluator of Helsinki University who evaluates the project and its pilot all the time.

## IV.   Resources

**4.1.**   **Human resources used**

Management level in the college, teachers, special teachers, vocational experts, psychologists, school nurses, social councillors and social advisors.

**4.2.**   **Organisational and technical means used**

Learning centre for learning difficulties, assessment procedures, minimum needs identification, regular meetings, multi-professional student welfare group.

**4.3.**   **Financial data**

Overall: ECU 260 000.
Operating costs: ECU 60 000.

## V.   Innovative features of the action

The results are innovative, because there has not been a systematic way to find out and identify the students' problems and needs, nor to encourage and help students with moderate learning difficulties to take courses in mainstream education, and in that way facilitate their chances of finding jobs and integrating into society and preventing potential dropouts. It gives practical tools for educational staff for improving the educational conditions and solving these student problems.

## VI.   Comments

# I. Brief description of the action

### 1.1. Name of the project
Youthstart — Integrating young people into work.

### 1.2. Organisation undertaking the action
Ministry of Labour and Ministry of Education.
Territorial: Apprenticeship office in Kotka.

### 1.3. Address
Ratakatu 14, 48600 Karhula.
City: Kotka. Country: Finland.
Tel: (358-5) 234 53 96. Fax: (358-5) 234 53 85.
E-mail: oppisopimustoimisto@kotka.fi
Contact: Pirjo Ranta.

### 1.4. Brief description of the action
The purpose of the project is to diversify vocational training systems, to offer alternative ways to those young people who are practical-orientated, and the intensification of the cooperation between the enterprises and educational institutions in apprenticeship training. Apprenticeship training means a job combined with a personal study programme. It includes on-the-job instruction and theoretical teaching of courses.

# II. Approach and content

### 2.1. Context, motivation and origin of the initiative
Long-term unemployed and uneducated youth may require new and more effective ways to begin vocational training. The goal of the Finnish Government is to develop and to expand special apprenticeship training for young people.

### 2.2. Target group
Young people under 20 years of age: vocational education, goal 3 250 persons.
Young vocational educated people under 25 years: further vocational education, goal 26 000 persons.

### 2.3. Socio-educational approach

### 2.4. Scheduling and length of the action
1996 to 1999.

### 2.5. Is your action/project in any way part of/supported by a national scheme or legislation that aims to combat social exclusion?

# III. Partnerships and means used

### 3.1. Name, status and role of the main partner

### 3.2. Other partners

### 3.3. Monitoring and ongoing evaluation

### 3.4. External evaluation of the action

**IV. Resources**

4.1. Human resources used

4.2. Organisational and technical means used

4.3. Financial data

**V. Innovative features of the action**

**VI. Comments**

# I.  Brief description of the action

### 1.1. Name of the project
Workshops for the unemployed youth.

### 1.2. Organisation undertaking the action
Turku City Municipal Youth Affairs, Ministry of education.

### 1.3. Address
Linnankatu 61 (Centre of Youth Affairs).
City: 20100 Turku. Country: Finland.
Tel.: (358-2) 262 31 11. Fax: (358-2) 262 31 28.
Contact: Tuuli Tuomi.

### 1.4. Brief description of the action
Sixteen workshops.

# II.  Approach and content

### 2.1. Context, motivation and origin of the initiative
Training to various professionals.

### 2.2. Target group
Socially excluded youth aged 17 to 25, unemployed for six months.

### 2.3. Socio-educational approach
Interviews and continuous help for lodging, further studies, network, etc.

### 2.4. Scheduling and length of the action
Six months for youths.
Two years for trainers.

### 2.5. Is your action/project in any way part of/supported by a national scheme or legislation that aims to combat social exclusion?
Project is financed by municipal and State funds.

# III.  Partnerships and means used

### 3.1. Name, status and role of the main partner
Administrations of Turku city (education, social affairs, health).

### 3.2. Other partners

### 3.3. Monitoring and ongoing evaluation
Continuous evaluation, statistics.

### 3.4. External evaluation of the action

# IV.  Resources

### 4.1. Human resources used
Nineteen trainers and their superiors at the workshops.

### 4.2. Organisational and technical means used
All the necessary technical equipment provided.

**4.3.    Financial data**
Youth affairs, FIM 1 million (this includes the rent of the workshop per year for services and materials FIM 500 000), FIM 6 614 458 for wages.


**V.    Innovative features of the action**
50 % of the trained youth have been employed after the project.


**VI.    Comments**

# I. Brief description of the action

### 1.1. Name of the project
Hämeenlinna Second Chance Pilot School.

### 1.2. Organisation undertaking the action
City of Hämeenlinna, Hämeenlinna Vocational Adult Education Centre.

### 1.3. Address
Hattelmalantie 25.
City: 13100 Hämeenlinna. Country: Finland.
Tel: (358 3) 614 71. Fax: (358- 3) 614 75 55.
E-mail: marjaleena.hulkko@hakk.htk.fi

### 1.4. Brief description of the action
The Hämeenlinna Second Chance School is a 'school without walls' where the vocational adult education centre is the core, the main site of all Second Chance activities. The Centre will receive young people under threat of exclusion, provide them with guidance and counselling and assistance to find training and employment possibilities. In their training path the trainees will follow personal curricula covering vocational studies in different educational institutions and will once in a while gather together in the Mother Centre to follow joint classes in information technology and languages.

# II. Approach and content

### 2.1. Context, motivation and origin of the initiative
Hämeenlinna Second Chance School is part of the Commission DG XXII experiment on combating exclusion thorough training and education.

### 2.2. Target group
Young persons 16 to 25 years of age, unemployed, perhaps school dropouts, insufficient qualifications, perhaps low marks hindering entrance to vocational education. Significant for the target group is that when they wake up in the morning they have no rational plans for the day.

### 2.3. Socio-educational approach
Learner centred and constructive learning approach, where the trainee takes responsibility for his actions. On-the-job learning will be emphasised and theoretical studies will be integrated in it. Also learning the transversal or core skills will be in the focus. Also the good practices of adult training and education will be benefited from.

### 2.4. Scheduling and length of the action
The pilot has started in 1997 and has duration of three years.

### 2.5. Is your action: project in any way part of/supported by a national scheme or legislation that aims to combat social exclusion
No.

# III. Partnerships and means used

### 3.1. Name, status and role of the main partner
Hämeenlinna Second Chance School is a hub-web approach where the local resources like educational establishments, local authorities dealing with young people and NGOs will develop their ways of working in the combat of exclusion. The enterprises of the region,

trade unions and employer organisations will support the pilot project in finding and offering vacancies, and looking for job placements in order to allow the youngsters to gain work experience.

### 3.2. Other partners
See above.

### 3.3. Monitoring and ongoing evaluation
The City of Hämeenlinna/City Council has set a steering committee to monitor the Second Chance School.

### 3.4. External evaluation of the action

## IV. Resources

### 4.1. Human resources used
The school will benefit from the existing teacher/trainer staff employed by the educational establishments in the city of Hämeenlinna. The Hämeenlinna Vocational Teacher Education College will run a training programme for Second Chance tutors who have been recruited among those working in the training organisations.

### 4.2. Organisational and technical means used
New technologies will form an important part of the curricula. Hämeenlinna Second Chance School will be included in the Intranet of European Second Chance Pilots and will develop approaches to benefit from the network. Young trainees will have access to PCs and will be encouraged to form relationships with their fellow students in other Second Chance Schools.

### 4.3. Financial data

## V. Innovating features of the action
The innovative nature of the Hämeenlinnna action is in the development and strengthening of local resources in the combat of exclusion. Also the approaches where young people will be the target of training/treatment, where adult training practices are benefited from are of an innovative nature.

## VI. Comments
Trainees will construct their own lives and future through different ways such as they have to take responsibility for their training and education, job seeking and employment. Personal tutors will support them and they will follow the developments though writing live stories and keeping personal diaries.

# France

## I.  Brief description of the action

### 1.1.  Name of the project
'Elite education for all'.

### 1.2.  Organisation undertaking the action
*La Bouture*.

### 1.3.  Address
19 Avenue Alsace, Lorraine 38000.
Town: Grenoble. Country: France.
Tel. (33-4) 76 51 25 62. Fax: (33-4) 76 51 25 62.
Contact: Bernard Gerde.

### 1.4.  Brief description of the action
Scheme for young people who have definitively dropped out of the upper levels of secondary school and are now seeking a second chance.
Designed as an information network using existing structures and combining the essentials of a public service with a network of partners which embraces both urban policy and the business world.

## II.  Approach and content

### 2.1.  Context, motivation and origin of the initiative
To provide an opportunity for those with a strong, if suppressed, motivation for education who have been excluded from school as a result of their own disruptive behaviour or have dropped out having convinced themselves that school is not for them.

### 2.2.  Target group
Young people who have completed lower secondary school and have given up in the first, second or third year of the upper secondary cycle (any type of secondary school) without completing the final year, and who are now seeking a second chance to obtain the *baccalauréat*.

### 2.3.  Socio-educational approach
'The *bac*'s not worth having, but without it you're not worth anything' is the line taken by these young people, who regret having left school but maintain that, at the time they took that decision, their own experience of school left them with no alternative.

### 2.4.  Scheduling and length of the action
Courses tailored to the trainee's experience to date and the nature of the project. Each new entrant is enrolled on an intermediate foundation course, followed by the modules

corresponding to the first, second and third years of upper secondary education, progressively leading to the *baccalauréat*.

**2.5. Is your action/project in any way part of/supported by a national scheme or legislation that aims to combat social exclusion?**

Participation in the 'Second Chance School' seminar held in Marseille in December 1996. Presentation of the project at the international symposium on the school dropout problem held in Lyon in January 1998.

## III. Partnerships and means used

**3.1. Name, status and role of the main partner**

National Education Authority.

**3.2. Other partners**

Industrial sponsors (Consignments and Loans Fund).
Grenoble Town Council.

**3.3. Monitoring and ongoing evaluation**

Advisory committee comprising seven university teachers and researchers (D. Glasman and J. Y. Rochex for education sciences, C. Jacquier and S. Roché for sociology, J. P. Simon and B. Darley for teaching methods, G. Wiel, *ADAGE*), plus two members of the teaching team.

**3.4. External evaluation of the action**

Under the supervision of the National Education Authority.
Special link with the IUFM.

## IV. Resources

**4.1. Human resources used**

Team of 15 members responsible for teaching, monitoring, mentoring, research/projects.

**4.2. Organisational and technical means used**

Suitable premises.
A computer system enabling certain training to be individualised.

**4.3. Financial data**

An operating budget expressed in teacher/hours covering the day-to-day accounts, as is usual in any other establishment. The industrial sponsors and the local authority cover additional costs occasioned by the organisation of workshops.

## V. Innovative features of the action

These young people are the rejects of the State education system, being no longer covered by the compulsory education arrangements. Their right to a second chance exists only in theory, as there are practically no public structures catering for them.

## VI. Comments

Genuine equal opportunities within State education are the aim of this ambitious project, which seeks to offer those referred to by Bourdieu as 'those excluded from within' [1] the means of finding a firm foothold in tomorrow's society.

---

[1] Free translation — no reference source given.

# I.  Brief description of the action

### 1.1.  Name of the project
Leonardo programme, Inserforpro project.

### 1.2.  Organisation undertaking the action
*Centre National d'Etudes et de Formation pour l'Enfance Inadaptée* (*CNEFEI*) (National study and training centre for maladjusted young people) Ministry of Education.

### 1.3.  Address
58-60 Avenue des Landes.
City: Suresnes – 92150. Country: France.
Tel.: (33-1) 41 44 31 22. Fax: (33-1) 45 06 39 93.
E-mail: cnefei@education.gouv.fr
Contact: Patrice Blougorn.

### 1.4.  Brief description of the action
Development of new media, guides, instruments for pupils and trainers (reference framework for social skills, CD-ROMs, films, training systems).
Joint organisation of training days for teachers and mentors in enterprises.


# II.  Approach and content

### 2.1.  Context, motivation and origin of the initiative
Establishment, reinforcement or re-establishment of a social link through job preparation.
Increasing interdependence between schools and businesses.

### 2.2.  Target group
Young people experiencing great difficulty at school — 14 to 18 years.

### 2.3.  Socio-educational approach
Promotion of key skills, primarily social skills.

### 2.4.  Scheduling and length of the action
Group work in Belgium, France, Greece and Sweden.
One transnational meeting per year.
Total duration of project: three years.

### 2.5.  Is your action/project in any way supported by a national scheme or legislation which aims to combat social exclusion?
Leonardo programme, Strand 1, Measure I.1.1.e.
Priority No: 3. Combating exclusion.


# III.  Partnerships and means used

### 3.1.  Name, status and role of the main partner
The CNEFEI, with its role in teacher training and research, is the project coordinator.

### 3.2.  Other partners
Sharing responsibility via a European network for the effective occupational integration of the least qualified.

### 3.3.  Monitoring and ongoing evaluation
Development of a timetable, development of products on the basis of social skills.
Reference framework — France, the project leader, will compile the consolidated report.

**3.4. External evaluation of the action**

In accordance with the Leonardo programme, regular compilation of a report and presentation of the finished products.

# IV. Resources

**4.1. Human resources used**

Twenty-two teachers (inspectors, head teachers, schoolteachers, etc.).

**4.2. Organisational and technical means used**

Use of school buildings and of the services of the Regional Centre for Educational Documentation (France) for the production of CD-ROMs, video facilities (Betacam film editing unit) in Sweden, etc.

**4.3. Financial data**

Estimate of the cost of the action:
- overall: ECU 382 446;
- when distinguishing various financial contributions and making available of technical and human means:
  — in investment terms: resources from Leonardo, ECU 156 908
  — in operating costs: resources from cofinancing, ECU 225 538.

# V. Innovative features of the action

The products may be considered innovatory in that they are the result of a process of applied research to promote vocational training measures for young people experiencing difficulties, in which businesses and schools work together and become integration cooperators.

# VI. Comments

# I. Brief description of the action

### 1.1. Name of the project
National and inter-regional education authority training systems for persons involved in measures to re-motivate young people aged over 16 years who have dropped out of school (CIPPA, SIO, MODAL, ITHAQUE — first year of integrated training).

### 1.2. Organisation undertaking the action
Ministry of Education.

Formation of a steering group from the General Office for Integration (*Mission Générale d'Insertion — MGI*) (IGEN — Inspector General for School Education; DESCO — Department for school education: initial, continuing and vocational training guidance service) — DAET, DAFCO, CSAIO, IA — Heads of establishments.

### 1.3. Address
MEN-DESCO A7.
City: Paris. Country: France.
Tel: (33-1) 55 55 22 60. Fax: (33-1) 55 55 21 41.
E-mail: tlegoff@men.fr
Contact: Anne Cousin.

### 1.4. Brief description of the action
Detailed examination of how these measures might possibly be updated by reviewing each other's teaching practices and producing a summary report for the use of those involved in the education system.

Use the work at these seminars as part of a dynamic drive on the part of those involved in the educational world to (re)establish themselves as participants capable of playing an active role in the school, social and occupational integration of young people.

# II. Approach and content

### 2.1. Context, motivation and origin of the initiative
Strengthen cohesion between the educational teams of the MGI.

Pooling of the skills of these teams from the moment of development and implementation of measures to re-motivate the young people in greatest difficulty in order to improve the clarity and effectiveness of measures.

### 2.2. Target group
Young people over 16 years of age who have dropped out of school and refuse to accept the 'rules' of school and working life, psychological and behavioural problems.

These young people are not enrolled at any school when they receive training in the context of MGI's measures.

### 2.3. Socio-educational approach
Assessment and analysis of the situation to find another way of obtaining the desired results.
Methodology based on the principle of research/action, aimed at giving a specific, operational response to the problems raised.
Development of a suitable methodology allowing those involved to form groups of centres of interest.

### 2.4. Scheduling and length of the action
1997/1998 school year.
Three national groups with a technical support group of instructors.
Six inter-regional education authority groups comprising heads of establishments, MGI education correspondents, instructors involved in the various measures.

**2.5.** **Is your action/project in any way supported by a national scheme or legislation which aims to combat social exclusion**

Application for ESF assistance for 1998-99 to help implement the measures, provide information about successful and innovatory measures, promote exchanges between those responsible at national level with a view to improving the quality of measures, and the publication of an introductory booklet by the integration office for those involved in the education system and external partners.

## III. Partnerships and means used

**3.1.** **Name, status and role of the main partner**

MEN/DESCO A7 — Coordinator of the measure — Organisation and support for the technical support group (12 people) — Back-up for all the seminars.

**3.2.** **Other partners**

Each group will have an 'observer' (teacher, researcher, inspector, permanent member of the committee on the local labour market, etc.), who will provide valuable opinions in assessing the work and creating the necessary openness towards partners.

**3.3.** **Monitoring and ongoing evaluation**

Report on the activity of each of the groups.
Seminar evaluation chart for participants.
Compilation of a summary report dealing with the organisational methods and innovatory measures for young people most in difficulty, implemented during the first half of 1999.

**3.4.** **External evaluation of the action**

Evaluation of the measures and numbers involved at national level by the Department for School Education and the Ministry of Education, Research and Technology's Planning and Development Department.
IGEN (report on occupational integration).

## IV. Resources

**4.1.** **Human resources used**

150 people took part in the various groups.

**4.2.** **Organisational and technical means used**

The six regional education authorities that organised the groups took responsibility for logistic matters (reception, accommodation, and rooms).

**4.3.** **Financial data**

Estimate of the cost of the action:
FRF 300 000;
- when distinguishing various financial contributions and making available of technical and human means:
  — in investment terms: 0
  — in operating costs: (travel expenses, accommodation, meals, rooms, etc.).

## V. Innovative features of the action

Study and development of educational projects with the various networks (regional education authority, departmental, local area).
Development of an organisation/training methodology backed up by the motivation of the group, research/action, training/action.

Perception of new career profiles to develop dynamic networks at national, regional education authority and local level.

Pooling the skills of teams of educational staff and encouragement of teamwork on the basis of specifications visible to all.

## VI.       Comments

These groups should make it possible to:

— recognise the skills of the staff involved in integrating young people experiencing difficulties into the education system;

— improved clarity and consistency of measures undertaken by all those involved in the education system and the partners (businesses, associations, local authorities, public networks for the integration of young people, etc.) striving for the social and occupational integration of young people.

## I. Brief description of the action

### 1.1. Name of the project
*L'école de la citoyenneté* ('school of citizenship'): *La Maison du Conte* ('the house of tales').

### 1.2. Organisation undertaking the action
*L'Association d'Animations Culturelles, Sociales et Pédagogiques La Contine.*

### 1.3. Address
La Contine, 153 chemin de Château Gombert 13013.
City: Marseille. Country: France.
Tel. (33-4) 91 95 96 01. Fax: (33-4) 91 95 96 01.
E-mail: lacontine@hol.fr
Contact: Agnès George.

### 1.4. Brief description of the action
The *La Contine* association provides training in secondary schools in Marseilles to prepare leaders and organisers of clubs to go into the neighbouring districts to put on their artistic productions before their peers, children and the population of the city. Our aim is to use the 'fairy tale world' theme to set up a local social centre managed by the active young members of the association in conjunction with teachers, story tellers, artists, social workers and senior citizens in the area. The young people are considered as players and not subjects.

## II. Approach and content

### 2.1. Context, motivation and origin of the initiative
The students would like to take on responsibilities and be recognised as individuals playing a role in getting society to change for the better. Marseilles has no 'fairy-tale world' for children; using tales makes it possible to arrive at a mix of generations and achieve a more amusing approach to reading and writing. Those involved in the life of schools (social assistants, educational advisers and counsellors) need help and backup in order to support their problem pupils more closely.

### 2.2. Target group
Secondary school students backed up by social assistants or interested in organising events with and for children, young people aged under 25 from the suburbs and other districts, nursery and primary school children, secondary school children, senior citizens.

### 2.3. Socio-educational approach
This teaching activity makes it possible to move towards a major sociological change, viz. the meeting up through cultural action of people of diverse ages and social circumstances. The oral tradition is once again used to good advantage.

### 2.4. Scheduling and length of the action
We will be following throughout a school year young people from different secondary schools during their free time thanks to the *Club Animation*, the training of club leaders and their own clubs already established. The young leaders are approaching the end of their school year and are placed in an organisational situation through the *fête des clubs*, a cultural and artistic event they are wholly responsible for organising (reception, safety, seeking out sponsors, publicity, shows, etc.). The events organised during the year by the active young members draw other young people from more disadvantaged circumstances who find in the association new friends who are positive-minded and provide encouragement.

**2.5.** **Is your action/project in any way part of/supported by a national scheme or legislation that aims to combat social exclusion?**

The *La Contine* project won a prize in 1997 from the *Fondation Caisse d'Epargne* in the context of its national campaign *Ensemble Contre l'Exclusion*.

## III. Partnerships and means used

**3.1.** **Name, status and role of the main partner**

The *Foyers Socio-Educatifs* of the Marie Curie and Denis Diderot schools in Marseilles have made available their premises and provide guidance for the trainees.

**3.2.** **Other partners**

The members of the national education authorities, events centres, social centres, training organisations (BAFA — *brevet d'aptitude aux fonctions d'animateur* (training for youth workers), *Secourisme et Brevet de Surveillant de Baignade* (training in first aid and lifesaving)), youth associations, artists, professionals and non-professionals from the show-business world, shopkeepers and businessmen.

**3.3.** **Monitoring and ongoing evaluation**

Supervision of each youth club, written reports on participants and training, questionnaires, films, artistic contributions at the *Fête des Clubs,* meetings, putting young people in an organisational situation.

**3.4.** **External evaluation of the action**

The trainers receive continuing training locally and through European training courses. This provides a critical view of action taken in order to devise a coherent strategy to make the association flourish.

## IV. Resources

**4.1.** **Human resources used**

Each member of the association is considered to be an active member taking part in the preparation of the *Maison du Conte*. At present, one trainer on her own voluntarily manages the whole of the training sector by involving young people who have already received training to provide help to the next group; professional players also provide assistance.

**4.2.** **Organisational and technical means used**

We are not well endowed in relation to the volume of demand. We have only one computer and no premises of our own to manage 20 youth clubs (involving 200 people) and organise a secretariat. We currently work in a network and have an office in the *Centres d'Animations de Quartiers municipaux* and in the *Foyers des Lycées*.

**4.3.** **Financial data**

Estimate of the cost of the action:

The network needs a basic budget of FRF 25 000 and the efforts of a few volunteers. In view of our success and in order to carry on our work efficiently, we would like to set up an *Antenne de Médiation Socio-Culturelle* to serve as our 'interface' office.

- overall: FRF 1 200 000
- when distinguishing various financial contributions and making available of technical and human means:
  - in investment terms: FRF 300 000
  - in operating costs: FRF 900 000 (inclusive of remuneration).

## V. Innovative features of the action

We are the first socio-cultural interface in Marseilles (linking up schools and districts). Our project for setting up a specific office (*Antenne de Médiation Socio-Culturelle*) for our purposes will enable us to establish *La Contine* as a 'local district arts school and social centre' along the lines of the community centres and what is organised by the national education authority.

*La Contine* is endeavouring to reconcile the members and players of the general (*Education nationale*) and adult (*Education populaire*) education bodies so that they can together meet the expectations of their public.

## VI. Comments

An increasing number of under-25s are requesting action by our organisation. *La Contine*'s work is centred on the idea of local identity and European identity, here again endeavouring to create a link and this is a strong attraction for young people looking for open-mindedness and new experiences. Respect, openness, joy, confidence, autonomy: *Contine*.

## I. Brief description of the action

### 1.1. Name of the project
*La Ville Pour Ecole* ('the city as a school').

### 1.2. Organisation undertaking the action
*Education Nationale Française.*

### 1.3. Address
121, 123 rue de Patay.
City: 75013 Paris. Country: France.
Tel./Fax: (33-1) 44 06 77 63.
E-mail: Ivpe@sancerre.ac-idf.jussieu.fr
Contact: Jacques Bonnisseau.

### 1.4. Brief description of the action
Return to school of young people excluded from the school system. The course is based on systematic tuition (learning by doing), a training boutique (getting up to the required standard through self-tuition), and a counselling workshop (better awareness of self as a basis for choosing one's options). The aim is to get every young person to define a training plan that is chosen and realistic, to regain lost confidence in himself/ and in the world around.

## II. Approach and content

### 2.1. Context, motivation and origin of the initiative
1. There is a need to meet a new demand for a school for young people who have 'no fixed school'.
2. There is a need to re-establish the links between the young person and the world around him (ignorance is often a source of many problems).
3. There are many other methods of learning in order to succeed.
4. Choosing one's pathway is essential (rather than being steered).

### 2.2. Target group
Young people aged 16 to 22, out of school or in the process of leaving without having completed it (those often referred to as dropouts). They are seeking a future, a place where they can be part of society after lower secondary school (in France). They are ready to become involved in their own training path.

### 2.3. Socio-educational approach
User-friendly structure in which the young person is a player and in which the supervision is based on assistance and counselling. Experience in the field is the basis on which to re-learn to learn and preparc a projcct. Thc arrangement is open to the city and to Europe (through the INEPS network of schools).
Preparation of a 'Portfolio'.

### 2.4. Scheduling and length of the action
The action will last up to one year depending on the date of arrival (enrolment possible during the year). Five cycles during the year alternating between three days per week of *in situ* training and two days at school. Gradual building up of a portfolio of skills in preparation for a feasible training project.

### 2.5. Is your action/project in any way part of/supported by a national scheme or legislation that aims to combat social exclusion?
The action is integrated into that of the Paris education authority focusing on the assistance and training of groups facing difficulties and is linked through the Lycée Jean Lurçat to the Lycée du Temps Choisi and the Lycée Autogéré de Paris. An application has been made under the Leonardo da Vinci programme.

## III.    Partnerships and means used

### 3.1.    Name, status and role of the main partner
National education authorities (*Education Nationale)*: secondary school premises, teachers and operational assistance.

### 3.2.    Other partners
*La Délégation Interministérielle à la Ville* (inter-departmental office for urban matters)
INEPS schools network.
*Réseau de Personnes Ressources pour les stages (*network of resource persons for training placements).

### 3.3.    Monitoring and ongoing evaluation
Training period record book (for follow up) (for personal use).
Portfolio (a booklet summarising the skills).
Worksheets and other material from the training boutique.

### 3.4.    External evaluation of the action
Multi-disciplinary team: conducting of surveys among young people, evaluation of the structure and its instruments, suggestions for improvement.


## IV.    Resources

### 4.1.    Human resources used
Three teacher-trainers including one psychologist and one person performing his national service in a civilian context.

### 4.2.    Organisational and technical means used
Multimedia resource centre, Internet connection (six computers).

### 4.3.    Financial data
Estimated cost of the action: FRF 500 000.


## V.    Innovative features of the action
Reception into a secondary school of excluded young people; tuition based on *in situ* experience even if this may have little bearing on a vocational qualification in the strict sense; basing counselling on better awareness of self; developing self-tuition; using all multimedia and communication resources; preparation for inclusion in an international network; involving young people and trainers in the management and development of the structure (being truly part of one's school and its history in and out of school).


## VI.    Comments
The INEPS network brings together many 'cities as schools' each adapted to its local and national context. Connecting them up to one another is a way of overcoming frontiers that are insurmountable at local level alone. It is a source of training and comparison, and of invaluable cooperation for trainers and young people alike.
The central idea of 'city as school' is to associate a number of innovatory arrangements in the same project and within the 'normal' education system. Differentiation at school is the answer to the wide range of emerging training needs.

# I. Brief description of the action

### 1.1. Name of the project

### 1.2. Organisation undertaking the action

### 1.3. Address
60 rue du marché.
City: Lille. Country: France.
Tel. (33-3) 20 78 21 13.   Fax:
E-mail: g.quinto@infonie.fr
Contact: Giuseppe Quinto.

### 1.4. Brief description of the action
Action pursued as headmaster in problem districts.
Action based on partnership with families, human rights and 'How to become a citizen'.

# II. Approach and content

### 2.1. Context, motivation and origin of the initiative
Children living in a very disadvantaged area strengthen my determination to make them fully-fledged citizens.

### 2.2. Target group
Pupils aged 6 to 12 mostly living in extreme poverty.

### 2.3. Socio-educational approach
I am in favour of involving singers/poets (J. Beaucarne, R. Lahaye), associations (*Mouvement alternatif non violent*), friends contributing their professional experience, people I meet (musicians, etc.), and observations made by children on the radio and television. This wide range of contacts makes for great open-mindedness.

### 2.4. Scheduling and length of the action
During my ten years as head of the school.

### 2.5. Is your action/project in any way part of/supported by a national scheme or legislation that aims to combat social exclusion?

# III. Partnerships and means used

### 3.1. Name, status and role of the main partner

### 3.2. Other partners

### 3.3. Monitoring and ongoing evaluation

### 3.4. External evaluation of the action

# IV. Resources

### 4.1. Human resources used

### 4.2. Organisational and technical means used

### 4.3. Financial data

## V.   Innovative features of the action

Placing the children in unforgettable and exceptional situations (visiting the Palais de l'Elysée, taking part in a live television programme).

## VI.   Comments

J. Beaucarne said 'My job is to tell you that anything is possible' and I have adopted that as my motto.

# I. Brief description of the action

### 1.1. Name of the project
Education and training in the fight against the exclusion of young people.

### 1.2. Organisation undertaking the action
Institut Jean Errecart.

### 1.3. Address
Institut Jean Errecart.
City: 64120 Saint Palais. Country: France.
Tel.: (33-5) 59 65 70 77. Fax: (33-5) 59 65 70 77.
E-mail: Institut.Jean.Errecart@wanadoo.fr
Contact: Marie-Dominique Desaegher.

### 1.4. Brief description of the action
Enhance the opportunities for integration for young people excluded from the labour market by securing for them the active involvement of local players (with the emphasis on work-linked training) and making available for them innovatory high-quality educational resources.

# II. Approach and content

### 2.1. Context, motivation and origin of the initiative
Our organisational profile (training centre situated in a rural environment) attracts an increasing number of young people who have dropped out of school, an event which is a factor of social and economic marginalisation and exclusion. They are the same ones whom we later find in integration-orientated schemes. What we do is to enable them to follow a normal school course, thus making it easier for them to enter working life thereafter. However, we also see that major social and family problems (serious financial difficulties, etc.) lead to early dropping out of school by certain young people who could otherwise have pursued a normal school career. Conversely, there is no getting away from the fact that certain youngsters are just not 'made' for the traditional school context and need a strong basis in day-to-day life. New, appropriately tailored pathways have to be thought up for these youngsters.

### 2.2. Target group
Thirty over-16s who left school with no qualifications.

### 2.3. Socio-educational approach
Teaching approach tailored to the needs, aspirations, aptitudes and level of development of the young person, and an active and constructive learning process for the pupil.
The aim is not merely to train young people but to integrate them firmly in society. The training programme will incorporate social integration activities.

### 2.4. Scheduling and length of the action
Each training pathway will last an average of at least one year, two years if possible, and will pursue three thrusts:
* basic skills: the tuition needed to bring the pupil up to secondary school level;
* vocational training: specific job-orientated training;
* in-company training prior to occupational integration.

### 2.5. Is your action/project in any way part of/supported by a national scheme or legislation that aims to combat social exclusion?
*Projet De Classe Clippa* (class intended to provide the students with certain foundation skills of learning) with the State and the regional authorities as partners.

## III. Partnerships and means used

### 3.1. Role of the main partner

Strong and durable partnership between the local authorities, the social services, associations and public and private sector companies, the latter being involved in defining the training pathway.

### 3.2. Other partners

### 3.3. Monitoring and ongoing evaluation

- Self-assessment of progress.
- Representatives of local firms will be involved in evaluation upon entry, at the half way stage and upon completion of the training period.

### 3.4. External evaluation of the action

Mentoring and tutoring.

## IV. Resources

### 4.1. Human resources used

Teachers of the Institut Jean Errecart and in particular the group of third and fourth-year technology stream trainers who have already had experience of helping and supporting young people in difficulty.

### 4.2. Organisational and technical means used

### 4.3. Financial data

Estimate of the cost of the action:
- overall: FRF 800 000/year;
- when distinguishing various financial contributions and making available of technical and human means:
  - in investment terms: FRF 150 000/year
  - in operating costs: FRF 650 000/year.

## V. Innovative features of the action

Emphasis on the learning of languages, particularly Spanish (proximity of Spain), of computer techniques (as a way of building up confidence), and of new technologies.
Work-linked training: in-company training to pave the way for occupational integration as a function of local strong points, viz. craft industry and commerce.

## VI. Comments

Work-linked training and apprenticeship are conducive to the acquisition of appropriate skills. Alternating in-company training and classroom-based training (at the training centre) would seem to be the best way of successfully rising to this challenge.

## I. Brief description of the action

### 1.1. Name of the project
Social and occupational integration of young people aged 16 to 25 facing difficulties: 'second chance' project.

### 1.2. Organisation undertaking the action
Université Paris XIII. Education science research group.

### 1.3. Address
Université Paris XIII, UFR Lettres et sciences humaines.
City: 93430 Villetaneuse. Country: France.
Tel: (33-1) 49 40 31 92. Fax: (33-1) 49 40 37 05.
E-mail: biarnes@lshs.univ-paris13.f
Contact: Jean Biarnès.

### 1.4. Brief description of the action
Setting up of an experimental structure (legal status: GIEQ — *Groupement d'employeurs pour l'insertion et la qualification*) which will:
1. create service jobs in the market sector;
2. provide the young people facing greatest difficulty with a wage generated by this work;
3. use this work as a basis for organising a 'training follow-up' for these young people;
4. get them into a skilled job or into training leading to a qualification;
5. be monitored by a multi-disciplinary research team with a view to sifting out aspects that can be transferred to other contexts.

## II. Approach and content

### 2.1. Context, motivation and origin of the initiative
Following up various lines of research, the university group's idea is to establish a partnership with 15 companies and focus in one forum the findings of this research. In particular, turning around the current integration policy approaches by first creating with these companies jobs which do not compete with existing jobs, training these young people by on-the-job work-shadowing using what they actually know in tandem with how their minds work and not how we think their minds work and what their deficiencies and shortcomings may be.

### 2.2. Target group
Young people aged 16 to 25 experiencing severe integration problems and not having the basic knowledge required.

### 2.3. Socio-educational approach
Person-focused constructive and interactive approach.

### 2.4. Scheduling and length of the action
Two years.

### 2.5. Is your action/project in any way part of/ supported by a national scheme or legislation that aims to combat social exclusion?
Supported by the DIIJ (*Délégation interministérielle à l'insertion des jeunes* — interdepartmental office for the integration of young people) and DG XXII.

## III. Partnerships and means used

### 3.1. Role of the main partner
Creation of the structure and subsequent analysis and evaluation of the action.

### 3.2. Other partners
Chamber of commerce, *Union Patronale* (employers' organisation), ANPE (national employment office), *Conseil général et régional,* DIIJ, DG XXII.

### 3.3. Monitoring and ongoing evaluation
Ongoing evaluation by a university research group (sociologists, psychologists, educational psychologists and historian) of socio-economic impact, of psychological and social changes, of trends among young people, of successes and failures in integration. Regular stocktaking, analysis of opinion, interviews and questionnaires.

### 3.4. External evaluation of the action
Chamber of Commerce.

## IV. Resources

### 4.1. Human resources used
In-company mentors, general trainers, professional training practitioners, and researchers.

### 4.2. Organisational and technical means used
Premises.

### 4.3. Financial data
Estimate of the cost of the action:
*   overall: FRF 750 000/year for 20 trainees (inclusive of wages).

## V. Innovative features of the action
Prior involvement of companies in a circumscribed economic area.
Creation of new jobs that do not compete with existing jobs.
Training young persons by on-the-job work shadowing using what they actually know in tandem with how their minds work and not on the basis of how we think their minds work or why we think they were previously unsuccessful.

## VI. Comments

# I. Brief description of the action

### 1.1. Name of the project
CIPPA: Period of work-linked training.

### 1.2. Organisation undertaking the action
Aix-Marseille regional education authority.

### 1.3. Address
City: F- 13621, Aix-en-Provence. Country: France.
Tel.: (33-4) 42 91 70 68. Fax: (33-4) 42 91 70 11.
E-mail: dact@aix.men.fr
Contact: Joelle Bruguière.

### 1.4. Brief description of the action
To help young people with no qualifications build a career plan and gain access to vocational training through an apprenticeship or resumption of studies leading to employment.

# II. Approach and content

### 2.1. Context, motivation and origin of the initiative
To prevent the exclusion of young people who leave the education system without acquiring sufficient general knowledge or occupational skills to integrate into working life.

### 2.2. Target group
Young people over 16 years of age who have failed at school, have no plans and are de-motivated.

### 2.3. Socio-educational approach
Giving young people the opportunity to succeed, and therefore re-motivating them: welcoming the young person as a human being, making the most of his achievements and skills, helping him discover the socio-occupational environment.

### 2.4. Scheduling and length of the action
Variable duration: from two to eight months.
Personalised training, backed up by periods of training in enterprises.
Implementation of the measure. Portfolio of skills for the recognition of achievements.

### 2.5. Is your action/project in any way supported by a national scheme or legislation that aims to combat social exclusion?
Action supported by the Ministry of Education.

# III. Partnerships and means used

### 3.1. Name, status and role of the main partner
Numerous local enterprises play a role in the joint training process.

### 3.2. Other partners
Protection judiciaire de la jeunesse (PJJ) (Judicial protection of young people).
Local offices.
FAS.

### 3.3. Monitoring and ongoing evaluation
Report compiled by the regional education authority.
Evaluation tools developed by the Ministry.

**3.4.** **External evaluation of the action**

In association with the partners.

## IV. Resources

**4.1.** **Human resources used**

Volunteer teachers for the personalised training, coordination and monitoring of each young person and supply teachers.

**4.2.** **Organisational and technical means used**

Organised by the regional education authority, regional authority organisation and monitoring group, infrastructure provided by schools.

**4.3.** **Financial data**

Estimate of the cost of the action: 43 CIPPA in the regional education authority = 950 young people involved:

- overall:
  FRF 3 800 000;
- when distinguishing various financial contributions and making available of technical and human means:
  — in investment terms: 0
  — in operating costs: human resources: FRF 1 145 000.

## V. Innovative features of the action

Personalised teaching approach in association with a network of partner enterprises.

Methods of recognising achievements adapted to the young people's background are particularly encouraging.

## VI. Comments

Results for the school year 1996/97:

4 % on fixed-term contracts/open-ended contracts;

34 % on apprenticeship contracts;

20 % preparing for the CAP (certificate of vocational aptitude) in vocational colleges;

30 % on work-experience programmes under the regional training plan.

# I. Brief description of the action

### 1.1. Name of the project
Preventing and remedying the school dropout problem.

### 1.2. Organisation undertaking the action
La Bouture.

### 1.3. Address
19 Avenue Alsace Lorraine 38000.
Town: Grenoble. Country: France.
Tel. (33-4) 76 51 25 62. Fax: (33-4) 76 51 25 62.
Contact: Bernard Gerde.

### 1.4. Brief description of the action
Increasing awareness among the public authorities and the general public of the situation of people dropping out of the education system.
Analysis of the dropping-out process.
Remedial action at all stages of the process — from disaffection to abandonment.
Organisation of symposia, seminars and training activities.

# II. Approach and content

### 2.1. Context, motivation and origin of the initiative
As trainers with the Mafpen (continuing training body run by the National Education Authority) we have, over the past few years, registered a pressing demand from teachers concerned with all forms of rejection of education from resistance to total abandonment.

### 2.2. Target group
Young people aged between 16 and 25 who are either on the point of dropping out of school on the grounds of mutual incompatibility, or have already dropped out and, having had a taste of the insecurity of a series of dead-end jobs, now wish to reconcile themselves with the system and complete their education.

### 2.3. Socio-educational approach
To start from the young person's current stages of development and build from there. Advantage is taken of the specific educational environment (adult teaching team plus mutually supportive peer group) and emphasis is placed on making demands as a way of boosting the trainee's confidence in his own potential.

### 2.4. Scheduling and length of the action
The association makes available specialised support services (social environment advisory committee concentrating on the dropout problem in schools, for example), takes action in local training markets and sets up training sessions of variable duration to meet specific demand.

### 2.5. Is your action/project in any way part of/supported by a national scheme or legislation that aims to combat social exclusion?
National programmes do not sponsor the project officially but the FAS (Social Action Fund) and INRP (National Pedagogical Research Institute) are supportive and provide funding on a one-off basis. We have applied for a European grant.

## III.  Partnerships and means used

**3.1.  Name, status and role of the main partner**

FAS, Grenoble municipal authority.

**3.2.  Other partners**

La Fondation de France; La Ligue de l'Enseignement.

**3.3.  Monitoring and ongoing evaluation**

Advisory Committee comprising seven university teachers and researchers (D. Glasman and J. Y. Rochex for education sciences, C. Jacquier and S. Roché for sociology, J. P. Simon and B. Darley for teaching methods, G. Wiel, *ADAGE*), plus two members of the teaching team.

**3.4.  External evaluation of the action**

Ongoing analysis of practices tested via the network (French and foreign partners, comparative studies, seminars, symposia, etc.).

## IV.  Resources

**4.1.  Human resources used**

Our association's members are drawn from all walks of education, from parents of pupils to heads of establishments, teachers, local authority policy-makers, etc.

**4.2.  Organisational and technical means used**

In 1998/99, the association intends to publish and distribute a liaison newsletter to partners within the network and potential users of its services (subject to the availability of funds).

**4.3.  Financial data**

An operating budget quoted in teacher/hours covering the day-to-day accounts, as is usual in any other establishment. The industrial sponsors and the local authority cover additional costs occasioned by the organisation of workshops.

## V.  Innovative features of the action

In France, where there is a real taboo on acknowledging the dropout statistics, taking any action at all in this field is an innovation. This type of action, attempting to combine the preventive and remedial approaches and networking national and international resources, is also innovative because there has been nothing in this field hitherto. The Lyon symposium held on 23 and 24 January 1998 was the first of its kind.

## VI.  Comments

We have also approached the IUFMs to convince them of the need for initial training to take on board the views of those who drop out of the education system, in order to ensure that their policies take account of the diversity of the school population.

# I.  Brief description of the action

### 1.1.  Name of the project
Integrated work-linked training (school/company sandwich training) in the clothing sector

### 1.2.  Organisation undertaking the action
Mission générale insertion — education nationale — Académie de Lille (lp *'Jacquard' Rue de la république, F — 59540 Caudry*).

### 1.3.  Address
*Mission générale d'insertion — Rectorat*
City: Lille. Country: France.
Tel: (33-3) 15 60 68. Fax: (33-3) 20 15 66 04.
Contact: Laurent Wattelet.

### 1.4.  Brief description of the action
Three-year work-linked placement, time being shared between a vocational secondary school and in-company training. During the first year the participant is considered to be a full-time pupil, whereas for the other two years he/she is considered as an employee under a training contract leading to a qualification.
Objective: provide preparation for the CAP (*certificat d'aptitude professionnelle*) with a view to occupational integration of young people who have failed at school.

# II.  Approach and content

### 2.1.  Context, motivation and origin of the initiative
Reconciling the requirements:
1.  of pupils, particularly those with no qualifications;
2.  of companies looking for trained manpower.
Locally, garment making attracts very few and only the lower skilled.

### 2.2.  Target group
Young people leaving SES. (*Section d'Education spécialisée des collèges*), the SEGPA (*sections d'enseignement général professionnel adapté*) or those who have failed in vocational training, those who are furthest removed from qualification and derive no benefit from existing VT structures and are not integrated in such structures.

### 2.3.  Socio-educational approach
Seeking the occupational integration of an unqualified segment by working in close conjunction with the business sector. The first phase consists of gaining familiarity with a profession through 'hands-on' experience.

### 2.4.  Scheduling and length of the action
Three years. A first year of observation (securing an agreement between the company and the young person), followed by two years of qualification (contract of employment).
The action is monitored throughout the three years by a coordinator working on a half-time basis.

### 2.5.  Is your action/project in any way part of/supported by a national scheme or legislation that aims to combat social exclusion?

## III. Partnerships and means used

### 3.1. Name, status and role of the main partner
The companies involved: providing familiarity with a profession through 'hands-on' experience. Direct or indirect involvement in training by identifying the points which need to be addressed at school. Recruiting.

### 3.2. Other partners
Consortia of companies, CCI, CIO (*Centre d'information et d'orientation*), GRETA (*Groupe d'Etablissements pour la Formation des Adultes*).

### 3.3. Monitoring and ongoing evaluation
A coordinator will devote half his time to monitoring, concentrating mainly on cooperation between the company and the vocational school irrespective of the status of the young person concerned and for whom the coordinator acts as the permanent point of reference.

### 3.4. External evaluation of the action
Contracts of employment.
CAP examination results.

## IV. Resources

### 4.1. Human resources used
Coordinator working on a half-time basis; in-company mentor; school teaching staff.

### 4.2. Organisational and technical means used
Based on the school's operational configuration; video.

### 4.3. Financial data
Estimate of the cost of the action:
- overall
  FRF 176 100;
- when distinguishing various financial contributions and making available of technical and human means:
  — in investment terms (human resources): FRF 166 350
  — in operating costs: FRF 9 750.

## V. Innovative features of the action
The typical pupil targeted by this action in an essentially rural context is unaccustomed to job-seeking, failure at school frequently being synonymous with 'staying at home'.
The action allows young persons to gradually take themselves in hand by providing them with work experience before starting on a course of training they previously thought themselves incapable of.

## VI. Comments
This action was instigated jointly by a businessman and a teaching team in order to also 'bring in' that segment of the population furthest removed from qualifications. The initiative is gradually modifying the education approach of the teaching staff to the greater benefit of the pupils.

# I. Brief description of the action

### 1.1. Name of the project
Territorial partnership and integration of young people.

### 1.2. Organisation undertaking the action
*AFP STAINS — Seine-Saint-Denis.*

### 1.3. Address
Boulevard Maxime Gorki.
City: 93240 Stains. Country: France.
Tel.: (33-1) 49 40 13  36. Fax: (33-1) 49 40 13  69.
Contact: Dominique Croisier.

### 1.4. Brief description of the action
Collaborative preparation of integration mechanisms bringing together training organisations, local departments, firms, to create a 'half-way house' between the world of young people and the world of business and industry.

# II. Approach and content

### 2.1. Context, motivation and origin of the initiative
The socially most advantageous bid clause under public invitations to tender in the *département* of Seine-Saint-Denis.

### 2.2. Target group
Young people aged 18 to 25 in the *département* of Seine-Saint-Denis marginalised (e.g. because of school failure, 'second generation' problems).

### 2.3. Socio-educational approach
The approach here is placed within an overall approach which takes due account of the requirements of firms and young people alike. The point for young people is to find their feet in a project focused on an appropriate job. The reality of the job offers them, within the arrangement, grounds on which to assert themselves. Having to face up to things, tangible acts as a fulcrum for socialisation, the consolidation of accepting oneself and the reactivation of the desire to learn.

### 2.4. Scheduling and length of the action
Recruitment on a joint basis by local departments, firms and training bodies.
Alternated prequalification phase.
Qualification phase under a contract opening on to a qualification.

### 2.5. Is your action/project in any way part of/supported by a national scheme or legislation that aims to combat social exclusion?
Action funded by the Île-de-France regional council on a cofunding basis with the ESF.

# III. Partnerships and means used

### 3.1. Name, status and role of the main partner
Provide the momentum for the collaborative preparation of integration mechanisms in accordance with the principles of mediation and transition.

### 3.2. Other partners
Firms: support, evaluation.
Local departments: social monitoring.

**3.3. Monitoring and ongoing evaluation**
Individual training record.
Consultation meeting of partners.

**3.4. External evaluation of the action**
Statistical monitoring of results by the party funding the action.

## IV. Resources

**4.1. Human resources used**
Coordinator/trainer, technical trainer, mentors, local department correspondents.

**4.2. Organisational and technical means used**
Conventional means: classrooms, workshops, in-company practical periods, in-company placements.

**4.3. Financial data**

## V. Innovative features of the action

Teaching framework straddling several institutions (firms, local departments, training bodies) thus creating a new forum in which the partners interact. This partnership-based system acts as a structuring element for the young people involved. The ability of the partners (who may not necessarily have the same values) to dovetail their work enables the young people to understand that continuity is possible between different worlds (young people's milieux and workplace).

## VI. Comments

A major attraction of the arrangement is the possibility of a job upon completion of the integration pathway.

# I.  Brief description of the action

### 1.1.  Name of the project
Social and occupational integration of young people who have dropped out of school.

### 1.2.  Organisation undertaking the action
*Service social des jeunes.*

### 1.3.  Address
27 Avenue de Ségur.
City: Paris 7ème. Country: France.
Tel: (33-1) 47 83 66 95. Fax: (33-1) 40 56 31  32.
Contact: Nathalie Harar.

### 1.4.  Brief description of the action
Taking charge of a group of 25 young people aged 16 to 18 who have dropped out of school and face the risk of marginalisation.
Restoring their knowledge base; teaching them how to become part of society; preparation of a personal and occupational plan for each of them.

# II.  Approach and content

### 2.1.  Context, motivation and origin of the initiative
The *Service social des jeunes* deals with a growing number of over-16s who have dropped out of school and face the risk of marginalisation.

### 2.2.  Target group
Young people facing the risk of exclusion: failure at school, dropping out of school at age 16 to 18; no plans for integrating society; problems at home and with their environment.

### 2.3.  Socio-educational approach
The approach here is centred on a multi-disciplinary team; teachers trained in education mediation techniques; personalised teaching monitoring; preparation of a plan for each one, backed up by tutoring.

### 2.4.  Scheduling and length of the action
One year for the basic learning process, followed in the second year by the introduction of individual projects.

### 2.5.  Is your action/project in any way part of/supported by a national scheme or legislation that aims to combat social exclusion?
Funding currently being sought from the *Conseil régional* and the European Commission.

# III.  Partnerships and means used

### 3.1.  Name, status and role of the main partner
Provide the momentum for a school for 16 to 18 year olds who have dropped out of school.

### 3.2.  Other partners
French: training centres; firms; social and education departments.
European: schools targeting the same group in Hungary, Denmark and Germany.

### 3.3.  Monitoring and ongoing evaluation
Continuous assessment: before and during the project, using texts.

Measurement of each young person's learning potential by a professional. Taking stock after two months.

### 3.4. External evaluation of the action
A Belgium university will evaluate our methods and their impact.

## IV. Resources

### 4.1. Human resources used
Multi-disciplinary team (psychologists, teaching specialists, guidance counsellors, tutors).

### 4.2. Organisational and technical means used
Premises capable of accommodating two groups of 12 young people. Rooms for cultural activities, multi-media rooms.

### 4.3. Financial data
Estimate of the cost of the action:
- overall: FRF 1.4 million;
- when distinguishing various financial contributions and making available of technical and human means:
  — in investment terms: 40 %
  — in operating costs: 60 %.

## V. Innovative features of the action
Taking full charge of young people who have dropped out of school and face the risk of exclusion; restoring their knowledge base using innovatory teaching methods (mediation). Development of intellectual potential. Teaching them how to become part of society. Preparation of a personal and occupational plan for each of them.

## VI. Comments
These young people in serious difficulty were previously taken charge of on an excessively piecemeal basis and therefore with indifferent results.

# I. Brief description of the action

### 1.1. Name of the project
Creation of an informatics workshop.

### 1.2. Organisation undertaking the action
*Association 'Pep 64'. Foyer pour adolescents 'le grand cèdre'.*

### 1.3. Address
64 Bd. Alsace Lorraine 64000.
City: Pau. Country: France.
Tel.: (33-5) 59 80 26 07. Fax: (33-5) 59 30 65 36.
E-mail:
Contact: François Banizette.

### 1.4. Brief description of the action
Developing access to the new communication technologies (Internet) as a way of integrating adolescents with social and occupational problems.


# II. Approach and content

### 2.1. Context, motivation and origin of the initiative
The future and the development of new technologies.
The establishment's (*'Foyer'*) mission of integration.

### 2.2. Target group
Young people aged 13 to 21 referred by the juvenile courts or the children's assistance organisation ASE (*Aide sociale à l'enfance*).

### 2.3. Socio-educational approach
The young people are brought into the context under the supervision of a youth worker.
Research/action.

### 2.4. Scheduling and length of the action
The workshop is open 12 hours weekly.

### 2.5. Is your action/project in any way part of/supported by a national scheme or legislation that aims to combat social exclusion?
In progress.


# III. Partnerships and means used

### 3.1. Name, status and role of the main partner
To be determined: funding arrangements.

### 3.2. Other partners
*Idem*: State/Regional Council/General Council/urban policy.

### 3.3. Monitoring and ongoing evaluation
Group of experts (sociologist, teaching specialist, etc.).

### 3.4. External evaluation of the action
See 3.3.

## IV.    Resources

**4.1.    Human resources used**
One youth worker and researchers (experts).

**4.2.    Organisational and technical means used**
Computer room equipped with the necessary hardware and software.

**4.3.    Financial data**
Estimate of the cost of the action:
- overall: FRF 250 000
- when distinguishing various financial contributions and making available of technical and human means:
  — in investment terms: FRF 104 000;
  — in operating costs: FRF 146 000/year.


## V.    Innovative features of the action
Three-year experimental project. Target group of anomic adolescents. The group will be assessed and possibly used subsequently for model building.


## VI.    Comments

# Germany

## I. Brief description of the action

**1.1 Name of the project**
Instead of school.

**1.2 Organisation undertaking action**
RAA der Stadt Essen (*Regionale Arbeitsstelle zur Forderung von Kindern und Jugendlichen aus Zuwandererfamilien*): regional agency for promotion of young people from migrant families in the city of Essen.

**1.3 Address**
RAA Essen.
Tiegelstrasse 27.
City: 45141 Essen. Country: Germany.
Tel: (49-201) 832 84 00. Fax: (49-201) 832  83 33.
Contact: Helmuth Schweitzer.

**1.4. Brief description of the action**
New learning schemes as 'second school': the aim is to combat younth unemployment through educating poorly qualified school dropouts.

## II. Approach and context

**2.1. Context, motivation and origin of the initiative**
Until now there is a lack of coordination/cooperation between schooling and social welfare institutions, counselling services in order to prevent youth unemployment and criminalisation.

**2.2. Target group (socially excluded youth, long-term unemployed, etc.; give ages and details of the populations concerned; their status)**
Socially excluded youth: 14- to 17-year-old pupils who refuse to attend school.

**2.3. Socio-educational approach**
To stabilise and strengthen the personality of the young people.
To develop social competencies.
To give individual support to the young people in qualified schooling, vocational orientation and preparing to the future employment market.

**2.4. Scheduling and length of the action**
Flexible scheduling and length (maximum two years) with an option to reintegrate in regular classes.

**2.5. Is your action/project in any way part of/supported by a national scheme or legislation which aims to combat social exclusion? Please describe**

It is an innovative project on regional level as part of a local network to prevent youth unemployment and social exclusion of the young people.

## III. Partnerships and means used

**3.1. Name, status and role of the main partner**

Local secondary school (*Hauptschule*).
Schools of special education (*Sonderschule*).
Vocational training schools (*Berufsschule*).
Vocational training and advice centres.
Municipal youth office.
They form an organisational network that is responsible for the project.

**3.2. Other partners**

Youth centres.
Mosques.

**3.3. Monitoring and ongoing evaluation**

A project action group consisting of representatives of main partners.
This group functions as a controlling agency.

**3.4. External evaluation of the action**

Only if it is financed.

## IV. Resources

**4.1. Human resources used**

Two teachers and one social educator.

**4.2. Organisational and technical means used (facilities, new technologies, etc.)**

Room for instruction and training including computer equipment.

**4.3. Financial data**

Estimate of the cost of the action:
— overall: DEM 366 000 per year;
— when distinguished various financial contribution and making available of technical and human means:
— in investment terms: DEM 10 000
— in operating costs: DEM 20 000.

## V. Innovative features of the action

An individual diagnosis of learning capacities and learning behaviour of the school dropouts and providing an individual schedule for them.
Establishment of a local network of all responsible agencies, which deal with the schooling/educating of socially excluded young people.

# I. Brief description of the action

### 1.1. Name of the project
Internet café.

### 1.2. Organisation undertaking the action
*Institut für Schulung und Beruf.*

### 1.3. Address
Wilhelm-Mangels-Str. 17-19.
Town: 56410 Montabaur. Country: Germany.
Tel. (49-2602) 90 65 00. Fax: (49-2602) 906 50 50.
E-mail: arno.scholten@t-online.de
Contact: Arno Scholten.

### 1.4. Brief description of the action
The 'Internet café' project is a set of measures aiming to provide stability, advice and help for young people in difficulty. The café is open to all, with no restriction on the use of computer terminals. It is intended to provide an initial point of contact between the young people and educational welfare workers who will attempt to persuade individuals to participate in an analysis of their own skills and aptitudes. This is followed up by motivation, training and occupational integration modules, all based around the computer, including such elements as innovative training, e.g. with the inf.-broker or jobs in a computer recycling centre.

# II. Approach and content

### 2.1. Context, motivation and origin of the initiative
Attempting to find jobs for disadvantaged young people in spite of the pressure on the labour market, without creating a situation of competition by trying to place them in the traditional sectors.

### 2.2. Target group
Young people in a situation of exclusion, i.e. those aged between 16 and 25 with no educational qualifications or vocational training and with no job or any prospects of finding one.

### 2.3. Socio-educational approach

### 2.4. Scheduling and length of the action
The project is for a unspecified period. Once the Internet café has been opened and enough participants have been found, the various measures will commence, offering scope for participation by newcomers. The duration of the measures will vary from 12 weeks to 12 months.

### 2.5. Is your action/project in any way part of/supported by a national scheme or legislation that aims to combat social exclusion?
No, but it will be supported by the local authorities and the employment exchange.

# III. Partnerships and means used

### 3.1. Name, status and role of the main partner

### 3.2. Other partners

**3.3.    Monitoring and ongoing evaluation**

**3.4.    External evaluation of the action**

## IV.    Resources

**4.1.    Human resources used**

Initially, three educational welfare workers, two teachers and one technician will work on the project. These numbers are expected to increase as the project progresses.

**4.2.    Organisational and technical means used**

**4.3.    Financial data**

Estimated cost of the project:
*    approximately ECU 320 000
     broken down by financial input and technical and human resources:
     —    investment, ECU 100 000
     —    operating costs, ECU 220 000.

## V.    Innovative features of the action

The innovative aspect of the project lies in its aim of finding openings for young people with no recognised educational or other qualifications in new and demanding occupational sectors. The essential principle is to combat exclusion not by finding openings at the very lowest level but by facilitating entry to high-status occupations, thereby giving the young people concerned a real and lasting chance of success.

## VI.    Comments

# I. Brief description of the action

### 1.1. Name of the project
FOQS.

### 1.2. Organisation undertaking the action
*Berufsfortbildungswerk GmbH (bfw).*

### 1.3. Address
Keithstraße 1-3 resp. Helmholtzstraße 2–9, 10587 Berlin.
City: Berlin. Country: Germany.
Tel.: (49-30) 392 60 96. Fax: (49-30) 391 30 46.
E-mail: 0303919635-0001@t-online.de
Contact: Rudolf Mondelaers

### 1.4. Brief description of the action
Bunch of 15 different classes.
Preparation of vocational training.
Preparation for taking a higher school degree.
General orientation.
Promotion of disabled participants.

# II. Approach and content

### 2.1. Context, motivation and origin of the initiative
High unemployment rate among young people in West Berlin in the beginning of the 1980s.

### 2.2. Target group (socially excluded youth, long-term unemployed, etc.; give ages and details of the populations concerned; their status)
Mainly young people between 17 and 25 years of age, who are unemployed, have no or not sufficient education and training for the job market.

### 2.3. Socio-educational approach
All courses and all participants have 'their' social worker. In addition there is a team of pedagogues specialised in certain spheres, such as law, debts, women and so on.

### 2.4. Scheduling and length of the action
The classes/courses usually last one year, starting at different times of the year.

### 2.5. Is your action/project in any way part of/supported by a national scheme or legislation that aims to combat social exclusion?
It is a part of the Berlin government's programme to fight the exclusion of young people (ARP) from others.

# III. Partnerships and means used

### 3.1. Name, status and role of the main partner
*Senatsverwaltung für Arbeit, berufliche Bildung und Frauen*
(Senator for work, professional education and women's affairs).

### 3.2. Other partners
Job centres in Berlin, providing the places with the job-creating programmes.
European Social Fond (ESF).

**3.3.** **Monitoring and ongoing evaluation**
Internet team conferences system (teams and sub-teams).

**3.4.** **External evaluation of the action**
Within the regulations of the European Social Fund.

## IV. Resources

**4.1.** **Human resources used**
Trainers (8), teachers (7), social workers (9), administration (2).

**4.2.** **Organisational and technical means used**
2 500 m² of training and teaching rooms and offices.

**4.3.** **Financial data**
Hard to tell as it has been built up over more than 15 years.

## V. Innovative features of the action
Starting in 1998
— information processing and telecommunication classes
— classes for video and sound editing.

## VI. Comments
FOQS consists of 15 different courses, which are independent, and only through their combination and putting together from FOQS with all its synergy effects.

# I.    Brief description of the action

### 1.1.    Name of the project
Integrative education and (vocational) training project for socially disadvantaged unemployed young people between the age of 20 and 25.

### 1.2    Organisation
*IFBE Institut für berufsbezogene Erwachsenenbildung GmbH.*

### 1.3    Address
Friedrichstaler Straße 39,
51645 Gummersbach,
Germany.
Tel.: (49-2261) 98 97-0. Fax: (49-2261) 98 97-60.
Contact: Lydia Pott.

### 1.4.    Brief description of the action
Depth analysis of skills, competencies and potentials; development of individual support plans with regard to school education, vocational training and social educational coaching; implementation of support plans in cooperation with local schools, chambers of commerce and crafts, potential employers (=local companies of all industries).


# II.    Approach and content

### 2.1.    Context, motivation and origin of the initiative
Origin of the initiative by the employment exchange office in Bergisch Gladbach.
Motivation: long-time experience with unskilled unemployed adults; wish to work with a prophylactic/preventive approach.

### 2.2.    Target group (socially excluded youth, long- term unemployed, etc.)
Socially excluded unskilled and unemployed youths between 20 and 25 with most heterogeneous socialisation deficits, total number  = 48 to 52.

### 2.3.    Socio-educational approach
Integral, i.e. considering all (potential) social partners of the youths.

### 2.4.    Scheduling and length of the action
Planned period of the project: 1 September 1998 to 31 August 2001, maximum period per youth: 12 months.

### 2.5.    Is your action/project in any way part of/supported by a national scheme or legislation that aims to combat social exclusion?
Prophylactic/preventive programme according to 'Sozialgesetzbuch III' by the Federal Labour Authority.


# III.    Partnerships and means used

### 3.1.    Name, status and role of the main partner
Employment Exchange Office in Bergisch Gladbach.

### 3.2.    Other partners
All schools in Gummersbach, Chamber of Commerce, local trade corporation, and approximately 50 companies in Gummersbach.

### 3.3. Monitoring and ongoing evaluation

Monitoring, continuous diagnoses and re-diagnoses via practically orientated assessment centres, reporting tools, written individual development report and statistical development control for the complete group.

### 3.4. External evaluation of the action

By Federal Labour Authority.

## IV. Resources

### 4.1. Human resources used

Two teachers, two experts in social education, three practical trainers within our training centre and practical trainers in the companies, one coach of the Chamber of Commerce.

### 4.2. Organisational and technical means used (facilities, new technology)

Two fully equipped classrooms, 12 fully equipped workshops within our training centre including high-tech laboratories.

### 4.3. Financial data

Overall DEM 1 800 000 for three years.
In investment terms approximately DEM 400 000.
In operating costs approximately DEM 1 400 000.
There is hardly any necessity in investing in special technical means because the workshops for our adult students can be used by the youth as well.

## V. Innovative features of the action

In our opinion the innovative feature of the action is our integral approach, i.e. it is the complexity of the project.

## VI. Comments

To date, school conditions are almost like laboratory conditions. If we aim at reintegrating disadvantaged young people into society, all parties of this society have to take over an active part in the education process.

# I. Brief description of the action

### 1.1. Name of the project
501/301.

### 1.2. Organisation undertaking the action
BBJ Servis gGmbH.

### 1.3. Address
Reichenberger Straße 36.
City: Berlin. Country: Germany.
Tel: (49-30) 616 85-501. Fax: (49-30) 616 85-600.
Contact: Ulrich Wisser.

### 1.4. Brief description of the action
Socially or otherwise disadvantaged young people not able to take part in other vocational training programmes or further education and are able to find a job of their choice, over a period of three years, where employment costs are covered by public finances. All support and assistance required to this end is integrated into the project

# II. Approach and content

### 2.1. Context, motivation and origin of the initiative
The amalgamated projects from West and East Berlin, called 501 and 301 respectively, provide an innovative solution in finding jobs and vocational training for young people who are difficult to place on the labour market

### 2.2. Target group (socially excluded youth, long-term unemployed, etc.; give ages and details of the populations concerned; their status)
Although provisionally based in Berlin, this project could be applicable in other regions having a similar socially disadvantaged target group of long-term unemployed young people aged between 18 and 27.

### 2.3. Socio-educational approach
A broad spectrum of advice and support is provided parallel to the placement, e.g. social care and job application assistance. Participants therefore gain middle to long-term employment perspectives.

### 2.4. Scheduling and length of the action
Individuals take part usually for a period of three years, after which permanent employment may be offered. After a five-year pilot project period of 501/301 the Federal Institute has now adopted 501/301 on a permanent basis.

### 2.5. Is your action/project in any way part of/supported by a national scheme or legislation that aims to combat social exclusion?
Yes, BBJ is commissioned by the Federal Institute of Employment under paragraph 23 of the Employment Support Law, and is financed by the Social Welfare Department from the Berlin Senate and the ESF.

# III. Partnerships and means used

### 3.1. Name, status and role of the main partner
Social Welfare Department — Berlin Senate responsible for the provision of financial support and project promotion activities.

**3.2.** **Other partners**
Regional Ministry of Labour, Berlin Senate Regional Employment Service, Chamber of Industry and Commerce, and training institutes.

**3.3.** **Monitoring and ongoing evaluation**
Research in the development of transferable elements of the project to regions with similar problems. Reports issued annually since 1993 with the help of software tools.

**3.4.** **External evaluation of the action**
Yes.

## IV. Resources

**4.1.** **Human resources used**
Socio-pedagogical support is offered in the form of social workers; vocational trainers who organise group-training schemes; and training provided by the employers themselves.

**4.2.** **Organisational and technical means used**
An administrative office is located in Berlin, serving as a point of contact for employers and participants, social workers, trainers and administrators.

**4.3.** **Financial data**
Estimate of the cost of the action:
*   overall
    DEM 38 000 per participant per annum
*   when distinguishing various financial contributions and making available of technical and human means:
    — in investment terms
    — in operating costs.
DEM 30 000: salary grants to employers, DEM 4 000; vocational training, DEM 4 000; administration (total participants: 700 per annum).

## V. Innovative features of the action
1.   'On-the-job' vocational training is combined with the necessary youth assistance and socio-educational support.
2.   Modular training enabling participants to gain qualifications on a step-by-step approach.
3.   Now in its 11th year, serves as model for long-term market integration.

## VI. Comments
Having been implemented in both east and west Germany, this project shows its adaptability to different societies and cultures. 501/301 tackles problems faced by regions throughout Europe and can be implemented not only in Germany, but also in other countries.

# I. Brief description of the action

### 1.1. Name of the project
*'Glashütte'* (14-18 years).

### 1.2. Organisation undertaking the action
*Arbeiterwohlfahrt*, Hannover.

### 1.3. Address
Arbeitwohlfahrt KV Hannover-Stadt. Marienstr. 14.
City: 30171 Hannover. Country: Germany.
Tel.: (49-511) 285 54-25. Fax: (49-511) 285 54-30.
Contact: Kristina Schmidt.

### 1.4. Brief description of the action:
Reintegration in society.
Motivation for pupils who refuse school.
Education in learning deficits.
Basic-qualification for work.
Cooperation with schools — teachers, headmasters, etc.

# II. Approach and content

### 2.1. Context, motivation and origin of the initiative
Initiative of youth/social-workers who were mobilised by reports that a rising number of schools are refusing to take certain categories of 'difficult' pupils.

### 2.2. Target group (socially excluded youth, long-term unemployed, etc.; give ages and details of the populations concerned; their status)
Pupils who have been victims of various forms of discrimination, aged from 14 to 18, without knowledge of German, lacking basic qualifications, suffering from a variety of social or behavioural 'deficits'.

### 2.3. Socio-educational approach
Individual teaching plan.
Working and learning in practical situations.
Work in youth-café, planning budget, home.

### 2.4. Scheduling and length of the action
For the pupils from six weeks, to one year on the action model for four years.

### 2.5. Is your action/project in any way part of/supported by a national scheme or legislation that aims to combat social exclusion?
Youth Helps which is a communal representation in cooperation of work Ministry for Schools and Culture, which is a decree dating from 1994.

# III. Partnerships and means used

### 3.1. Name, status and role of the main partner
1. Youth office Hannover (planning the action of youth-social-works).
2. Ministry for Schools and Culture.

### 3.2. Other partners
Labour offices.
Professional helpers from city districts.

**3.3.    Monitoring and ongoing evaluation**

At this time only communal monitoring — youth office.

Evaluation is part of youth-social-planning in the town of Hannover

**3.4.    External evaluation of the action**

Only in planning with Ministry of Schools and Culture.

## IV.    Resources

**4.1.    Human resources used**

The project is now starting with one guardian and four social workers (10 hours a week).

**4.2.    Organisational and technical means used**

Workshops with tools, personal computers.

**4.3.    Financial data**

Estimate of the cost of the action:

- overall
  for four years, DEM 1 000 000;
- when distinguishing various financial contributions and making available of technical and human means:
    — in investment terms: DEM 22 500.
    — in operating costs
      personnel: DEM 200 000 a year
      Others: DEM 60 000 a year.

## V.    Innovative features of the action

Project has brought practices of discrimination in school entrance policies to the surface.

## VI.    Comments

The project is at this time in a preliminary phase.

The finance is not yet cleared up.

There is a political pressure to start the project immediately.

# Greece

## I. Brief description of the action

### 1.1. Name of the project
A pilot programme on the vocational training of young people who failed to complete their basic school education.

### 1.2. Organisation undertaking the action
National Labour Institute.

### 1.3. Address
6-8 K. Palama Str.
City: 111 41 Athens. Country: Greece.
Tel: (30-1) 211 19 06-7. Fax: (30-1) 228 51 22.
E-mail: etheodo@eie.org.gr
Contact: Helen Theodoropoulos.

### 1.4. Brief description of the action
This project includes:
Elaboration of a training model based on the virtual application (assimilation) of various scenarios on training and rehabilitation of school dropouts and the under-qualified, of up to 22 years.
Based on the results obtained from assimilation, experimental implementation of the best scenario, in a pre-selected area.
The project also suggests the introduction of: (a) a special allowance and/or training coupon of an alternative use for work placement and, (b) a special work permit for the under aged.

## II. Approach and content

### 2.1. Context, motivation and origin of the initiative
The actions described above, constitute a concrete response to the general orientation and high sensibility reflected in Ministry of Labour policy, as to the problems of improving employability, especially for the young, and preventing social exclusion.
The need for activation on those fields is also being highlighted by the EU employment guidelines for 1998.

### 2.2 . Target group (socially excluded youth, long-term unemployed, etc.; give ages and details of the populations concerned; their status)
The project proposed, mainly addresses dropout, under-age workers and, more generally, young people of up to 22 years, who have failed to complete compulsory education, and refuse to re-enter the education system.

### 2.3. Socio-educational approach

It is true that the problem of early school leavers is partly connected to the deficiencies of the educational and training system, which fails to catch up with the pace of development, and provide qualifications that would respond to the demands of the world of the market. The recent Law 2525/97, on the reform of education and training systems, constitutes a significant step towards the adaptation of education and training to the labour market needs.

Also, the model of apprenticeship schools. Applied by the national employment service (OAED) since many years now, attempts to better link training to real working conditions. The young unemployed, and particularly those with no formal qualifications, have been identified by the new employment policy principles, as a 'high risk group', threatened by long-term unemployment and therefore, exclusion. The risk is aggravated by the fact that, in most cases, early school leavers originate from very low socio-economic and cultural environments, and continue to feel more and more marginalised and unable to follow the rest of society, as the possibility is denied to them to develop their personality and skills. For all those reasons, this proposal was drawn up with the ambition to constitute an innovative step forward, aimed at the prevention of social exclusion for a particular and very sensitive group of young people, by helping them, timely enough, to find their way into the labour market.

### 2.4. Scheduling and length of the action

The realisation of the project is planned to extend to one year, over which, the various actions have been scheduled:

Collection of information — redaction of questionnaires (two months), elaboration of the data obtained — codification (6m), development of model and training programme — assimilation (5m), pilot application (4m), evaluation — conclusions (4m).

### 2.5. Is your action/project in any way part of/supported by a national scheme or legislation that aims to combat social exclusion? Please describe

The action will be funded and supported by the Ministry of Labour and Social Security as a part of a more general action to combat and prevent social exclusion.

## III. Partnerships and means used

### 3.1. Name, status and role of the main partner

The National Labour Institute (NLI) is a private law research institution, which has been established on the initiation of social partners and the Ministry of Labour with the support of the European Commission. NLI is supervised by the Ministry of Labour and Social Security and it will be the main actor, responsible for the implementation and coordination of the actions.

### 3.2. Other partners

For the realisation of the actions, the NLI is going to work in close cooperation with the national employment service (OAED) and other research institutions, such as the Pedagogical Institute, for the gathering of information, the use of already existing data bases, the realisation of the training actions, etc.

### 3.3. Monitoring and ongoing evaluation (monitoring, reporting tools, etc.)

The EIE will be responsible for the on-going evaluation of the project evolution, registering and periodically reporting on the results of each phase accomplished.

### 3.4. External evaluation of the action

Responsible for the external evaluation will be the Ministry of Labour and Social Security.

## IV. Resources

### 4.1. Human resources used (teachers, guardians, etc.)

For the implementation of the actions, a number of scientific collaborators and experts will be used, in various specialties, such as: sociologists, statisticians, economists, research assistants, etc.

### 4.2. Organisational and technical means used

The facilities and technical equipment already existing at the EIE and other institutions (i.e. OAED schools) will largely be used for the realisation of the actions.

### 4.3. Financial data

Estimate of the cost of the action:

Overall: GRD 16 710 000 (ECU 47 472).

When distinguishing various financial contributions and making available of technical and human means:

—  in investment terms: GRD 14 110 00  (ECU 40 085)
—  in operating costs: GRD 2 600 000 (ECU 7 387).

## V. Innovative features of the action

Although the problem of dropouts and under-age workers has been quite important in many regions of Greece, including specific areas of Athens, the existing legal frame addressing those persons is still to be completed.

This project wishes to contribute, setting the parameters for the creation of those legal schemes that will efficiently protect this group of young workers.

Such could be the case of the training — work permit suggested.

Furthermore, the training coupon will introduce flexibility to the conditions under which the young, under-qualified people work, by helping them remain in the labour market while being trained in a field relevant to their occupation, or choose to just be trained in any other field of their own preference.

Finally, through registering the particular needs of the specific area where the pilot application is to be carried out, the project will respond in a more concrete and 'material' way to specific problems of the individuals concerned.

## VI. Comments

# I.    Brief description of the action

### 1.1.    Name of the project
'Youth Support Centres'.

### 1.2.    Organisation undertaking the action
ARSIS (association for the social support of youth).

### 1.3.    Address
Ê. Loukareos 15, Athens 11475, Greece,
Tel./Fax: (30) 644 21 98, 642 46 03.
E-mail: arsisath @ compulink.gr.
Contact: Katerina Poutou.

### 1.4.    Brief description of the action
Through Youth Support Centres, ARSIS provides support for social and vocational integration to young people aged 15 to 21, who have experienced conflict, neglect, school failure, or various forms of social exclusion. The services operate on a multidimensional base, offering simultaneously personal advice and support, vocational preparation and creative leisure activities. Nowadays there are three YSC run by ARSIS in Athens, Thessaloniki and Volos.

# II.    Approach and content

### 2.1.    Content, motivation and origin of the initiative
The centres' services have so far been mostly associated with paid vocational training programmes but gradually they become more independent. The initiative started in 1992, attempting to act as an example to fill in serious gaps in social protection policies for disadvantaged and marginalised youth in Greece.

### 2.2.    Target group
Socially excluded youth aged 15 to 21 (occasionally up to 23), who have been through penal justice, have dropped out of school, are homeless, belong to disadvantaged minorities or face serious problems in their living environments. The target group is widened as far as creative and recreational activities are concerned: any young person from the local communities is welcomed to participate.

### 2.3.    Socio-educational approach
ARSIS attempts to socialise and strengthen young people, so that they become more self-confident and capable of finding solutions and making responsible decisions concerning participation in social and economic life. All activities are based on free will participation and on common agreements.

### 2.4.    Scheduling and length of the action
The Youth Support Centres may operate all year long (if funds are available) and a young person may use its services from a one-day appointment up to unlimited time. However, usually training programmes last three to six months, and young persons participate in various activities or use services regularly for no longer than two years.

### 2.5.    Is your action/project in any way part of/supported by a national scheme or legislation which aims to combat social exclusion?
The YSCs receive some support by the European Commission and the Greek Government (General Secretariat for Youth), through the European Employment Initiative and the structural funds against exclusion from the labour market.
However this support is not sufficient to allow their full operation.

# III. Partnerships and means used

**3.1. Name, status and role of the main partner**

The General Secretariat for Youth (belongs to the Ministry of Education) is a partner and co-funder of many activities of ARSIS in the YSCs.

**3.2. Other partners**

The General Secretariat for Popular Education.
Municipal companies and training centres.
The National Agency for Local Government and Development.
The Society for the Care of Minors.

**3.3. Monitoring and ongoing evaluation**

Internal system created by the scientific documentation section of ARSIS.

**3.4. External evaluation of the action**

It lies on the responsibility of funding agencies but so far has not been enforced.

# IV. Resources

**4.1. Human resources used**

Social workers, vocational orientators, youth workers, lawyers, animators, specialists trainers, trained volunteers.

**4.2. Organisational and technical means used (facilities, new technology, etc.)**

Small-scale projects based in buildings of around 150-200 m$^2$.
Three buildings available in Athens, two buildings in Thessaloniki and one building in Volos.
P.C., printers, access to Internet available.

**4.3. Financial data**

Estimate of the cost of the action
Athens: GRD 30-40 000 000 per year;
Thessaloniki: GRD 20-25 000 000 per year;
Volos: GRD 10-15 000 000 per year;
Overall: GRD 40-80 000 000 per year.

# V. Innovative features of the action

This is a very innovative project, as it introduces new models of educational and social work with young dropouts, through processes which are associated with the involvement and cooperation among public agencies, local government and non-governmental organisations.

# VI. Comments

Despite its innovative character, the project of ARSIS has not managed so far to ensure stable national State funding, as the existing institutional framework for educational or social policies would not easily allow this. It is hoped that in the future similar projects will be able to receive stable recognition and support.

# I. Brief description of the action

### 1.1. Name of the project
Elefsina: An integrated approach.

### 1.2. Organisation undertaking the action
Institute of training and vocational guidance (IEKEP).

### 1.3. Address
34A Averoi str, 142 32 N. Ionia.
City: Athens. Country: Greece.
Tel.: (30-1) 218 69 70; 218 69 71. Fax: (30-1) 218 69 72.
E-mail: IEKEP@HOL.GR
Contact: Pinepoli Stathakopoulos.

### 1.4. Brief description of the action
Social and vocational integration of disadvantaged young people on the local level by using the community development approach.

# II. Approach and content

### 2.1. Context, motivation and origin of the initiative
Elefsina is a region facing serious social and economic problems due to the effects of de-industrialisation. As a result, there is a high rate of unemployment in the region together with a high rate of school dropouts (about 40 %).

### 2.2. Target group (socially excluded youth, long-term unemployed, etc.; give ages and details of the populations concerned; their status)
Disadvantaged young people, 16- to 25-years-old who have abandoned compulsory education and/or do not have qualifications.

### 2.3. Social approach
The community development approach is a method of intervention within the context of community social work. It is through consensus, citizen participation and coordination of the involved social partners that social problems at the local level are being dealt with.

### 2.4. Scheduling and length of the action
The use of the community development approach in Elefsina began in 1995 with Cedefop's Action Research Project 'Social and Occupational Integration of Young People at Local Level'. Following that, and within the framework of Initiative Employment—Youthstart, we implemented in Elefsina a 150-hours workshop for 10 young people, 16- to 18-years-old, using alternative pedagogical methods with the purpose of assisting their integration into the educational system or the labour market. This effort is continuing within the framework of a Leonardo da Vinci project, 'Cooperation at Local Level'.

### 2.5. Is your action/project in any way part of/supported by a national scheme or legislation that aims to combat social exclusion?
Our work in Elefsina began with Cedefop's Action Research, continued with Employment Initiative Youthstart and our intervention proceeds through a Leonardo da Vinci project 'Cooperation at Local Level'.

## III. Partnerships and means used

### 3.1. Name, status and role of the main partner

IEKEP is a non-profit organisation that has an expertise in community development, vocational guidance and training. IEKEP's role is that of the project coordination and animator.

### 3.2. Other partners

Hellenic Manpower organisation, public schools, social agencies.

### 3.3. Monitoring and ongoing evaluation

Regular meetings of the local committee 'animated' by IEKEP. Regular reports.

### 3.4. External evaluation of the action

There is no external evaluator.

## IV. Resources

### 4.1. Human resources used

Trainers, teachers, social workers, administrators, guidance officers.

### 4.2. Organisational and technical means used (facilities, new technology)

### 4.3. Financial data

It cannot be estimated because the action has resources from various projects.

## V. Innovative features of the action

Community development approach used for the social and occupational integration of young people. The use of alternative pedagogical methods.
The use of a computer assisted vocational guidance tool.

## VI. Comments

It is worth mentioning that the action described is not a training one, hence some of the questions do not seem appropriate.

# I. Brief description of the action

### 1.1. Name of the project
Centres of Working Youth.

### 1.2. Organisation undertaking the action
Working Fellowship Organisation.

### 1.3. Address
10 Agisilaov str.
City: Athens. Country: Greece.
Tel: (30-1) 522 02 64. Fax: (30-1) 524 61 89.
Contact: A. Angyropoulou.

### 1.4. Brief description of the action
The centres for working youth aim at: 1. training, 2. entertaining, 3. giving information about contemporary social problems.

# II. Approach and content

### 2.1. Context, motivation and origin of the initiative
The 41 centres for working youth, spread all over Greece, started operating in 1970 in industrial areas. Their main target was to support employees through their programmes.

### 2.2. Target group (socially excluded youth, long-term unemployed, etc.; give ages and details of the populations concerned; their status)
Disadvantaged young people, 16- to 25-years-old who have abandoned compulsory education and/or do not have qualifications.

### 2.3. Socio-educational approach
The centres for working youth offer courses based on indoor training.

### 2.4. Scheduling and length of the action
The centres for working youth offer long-term courses.

### 2.5. Is your action/project in any way part of/supported by a national scheme or legislation, which aims to combat social exclusion?
The programmes of Working Fellowship Organisation are financed by employees' and employers' contributions.

# III. Partnerships and means used

### 3.1. Name, status and role of the main partner
The centres for working youth are open for employees and their family members aged from 9 to 32 years under the condition of contributing to the Working Fellowship Organisation. The Ministry of Labour and Social Insurance supervises the Working Fellowship Organisation

### 3.2. Other partners
An 11-member board (employees, the political head of supervising ministry and employees of the organisation) manages the Working Fellowship Organisation.

**3.3.** **Monitoring and ongoing evaluation**

The working fellowship programme is supervised and evaluated by the Ministry of Labour and Social Insurance.

**3.4.** **External evaluation of the action**

The Working Fellowship Organisation is not under any other evaluation.

## IV. Resources

**4.1.** **Human resources used**

Administrators, trainers, teachers, social workers, helping personnel.

**4.2.** **Organisational and technical means used**

**4.3.** **Financial data**

It cannot be estimated because the action has resources from various projects.

## V. Innovative features of the action

Used for the social and occupational integration of young people.
The use of a computer assisted vocational guidance tool.

## VI. Comments

# Ireland

## I. Brief description of the action

### 1.1. Name of the project
The Vocational Training Opportunities Scheme (VTOS).

### 1.2. Organisation undertaking the action
The Department of Education and Science, Ireland.

### 1.3. Address
The Adult Education Section, Department of Education and Science, Floor 11, Hawkins House, Hawkins St.
City: Dublin. Country: Ireland.
Tel.: (353-1) 873 47 00. Fax: (353-1) 671 52 70.
Contact: Helen Keogh, c/o CDU, Sundrive Rd, Dublin 12. Tel.: (353-1) 453 54 87. Fax: (353-1) 453 76 59.
E-mail: helen.keogh@cdu.cdvec.ie

### 1.4. Brief description of the action
VTOS is an ESF-supported second-chance vocational education and training initiative to enable unemployed people aged 21+ years and on the Live Register of Unemployment for a minimum of six months to return to full-time learning at a wide range of levels and in a wide range of areas. They obtain national certification that enables them to proceed to employment or self-employment directly or indirectly, through further education/training.

## II. Approach and content

### 2.1. Context, motivation and origin of the initiative
Since 1989, VTOS seek to address the very low levels of vocational and educational qualifications among long-term unemployed people in Ireland — up to 80 % do not hold a Leaving Certificate or other qualification (the certificate achieved by 18-year olds at the end of upper secondary education) which is a basic requirement nowadays for entry to the majority of occupations.

### 2.2. Target group
Some 5 000 places nationally for unemployed people aged at least 21 years of age and on the Live Register of unemployment for a minimum of six months. 10 % of places are available to a broader category of unemployed people, including lone parents, people in receipt of disability allowances and the spouses of people eligible to join the scheme.

### 2.3. Socio-educational approach
VTOS seeks to promote social inclusion for unemployed people (and their families) by enabling them to re-integrate in the labour market through gaining worthwhile national

qualifications, by enabling them to develop self-esteem and confidence as individuals, members of families, workers and members of communities, and by giving them opportunities to participate in a wide range of activities and environments from which unemployed people are often effectively excluded.

### 2.4. Scheduling and length of the action

VTOS began in 1989 with approximately 280 participants and it now offers 5 000 places each year in 94 centres nation-wide. Programmes under the Initiative last up to two years full-time and people who enter at a very low level of educational achievement may participate for three years in all.

### 2.5. Is your action/project in any way part of/supported by a national scheme or legislation which aims to combat social exclusion? Please describe

VTOS form part of the national response to social exclusion represented by initiatives/actions such as the National Anti-Poverty Strategy (NAPS); the local area-based partnership approach to unemployment and local development; the Operational Programme for Human Resource Development.

## III. Partnerships and means used

### 3.1. Name, status and role of the main partner

The Department of Education and Science, Ireland; Government department with responsibility for the education system.

### 3.2 Other partners

The Department of Social, Community and Family Affairs; the 33 Vocational Education Committees (VECs) (local vocational education authorities).

### 3.3. Monitoring and ongoing evaluation

Monitored by the Monitoring Committee for the Operational Programme for Human Resources Development; by the Human Resources Coordination Committee; by the Department of Education and Science (ESF), and adult education sections; by the VTOS National Coordinator; by the VECs.
On-going evaluation — at VTOS centres and VEC level; at national Departmental level.

### 3.4. External evaluation of the action

Evaluation commissioned by the Department of Education (WRC Social and Economic Consultants 1994); mid-term evaluation of the Human Resources Development Operational Programme 1994-99 (Goodbody Economic Consultants 1997); current evaluation being undertaken by the ESF Evaluation Unit of the Department of Enterprise, Trade and Employment.

## IV. Resources

### 4.1. Human resources used

Up to 600 tutors/trainers throughout the country in vocational schools and adult education centres; 40 adult education organisers.

### 4.2. Organisational and technical means used

VTOS participants are accommodated in vocational schools and in adult education centres throughout Ireland. The vast majority of the schools/centres are equipped with ICTs and many of them, depending on the courses offered, provide specialist rooms for a wide range of vocational designations.

### 4.3. Financial data

Estimate of the cost of the action:

Overall — Approximately IRP 25 million per annum (Department of Education and Science with assistance from the European Social Fund).

## V.  Innovative features of the action

VTOS has put in place a crucial phase of lifelong learning in that it enables unemployed people aged 21+ with low levels of educational and vocational qualifications to resume their learning on a full-time basis for up to two years (most typically) and to achieve a wide range of national educational and vocational qualifications. The project is guided by a person-centred approach.

## VI.  Comment

The Department of Education and Science have just published a book of 103 success stories from VTOS entitled 'VTO Spells Success'.

# I.  Brief description of the action

### 1.1.  Name of the project
Integrated Development of Designated Disadvantages and Other Areas (Sub-programme 2 of the Local Urban and Rural Development Operational Programme).

### 1.2.  Organisation undertaking the action
Area Development Management Ltd is the intermediary company with overall responsibility for managing the programme operated by 38 Area Partnerships and 33 funded Community Groups.

### 1.3.  Address
Holbrook House, Holles Street.
City: Dublin 2. Country: Ireland.
Tel.: (01) 661 36 11. Fax: (01) 661 04 11.
E-mail: admltd@iol.ie
Contact: Joan Walsh.

### 1.4.  Brief description of the action:
The LURD OP consists of three sub-programmes — ADM Ltd has responsibility for the programme on integrated development of designated disadvantages areas. The funded organisations prepare and implement local development plans, which include education actions, designed to prevent early school leaving and which also offer second chance education and training.

# II.  Approach and content

### 2.1.  Context, motivation and origin of the initiative
The LURD OP constitutes one of the four priorities in the CSF 1994-99 agreed by the Irish Government and the Commission of the EC.  It is designed to bring about social and economic development at local level.

### 2.2.  Target group (socially excluded youth, long-term unemployed, etc.; give ages and details of the populations concerned; their status)
People who are socially excluded, long-term unemployed or those at risk of becoming long-term unemployed. Education actions are targeted at young people at all levels of the education system and at unemployed adults.

### 2.3.  Socio-educational approach
1.  Prevention of under-achievement and facilitation of participation in the education system through complementary or supplementing mainstream provision and also through developing innovative approaches.
2.  Providing 'second-chance' education and training, through increasing accessibility to mainstream course provision of specific courses, promoting integration into the labour market.

### 2.4.  Scheduling and length of the action
The programme is from 1994 to 1999 and individual actions are of varying duration.

### 2.5.  Is your action/project in any way part of/supported by a national scheme or legislation that aims to combat social exclusion?
It is a sub-programme of the Operational Programme on Local Urban and Rural Development, part of the CSF for Ireland 1994-99, as such it forms part of the national strategy to combat social exclusion.

## III. Partnerships and means used

### 3.1. Name, status and role of the main partner
Not directly applicable, however, at national level the Department of Education supports the education measure of the programme at local level, various consortia of partners are developed.

### 3.2. Other partners
Between partnership companies, local schools, youth organisations, parent organisations.

### 3.3. Monitoring and ongoing evaluation
Each funded organisation conducts its own evaluation. ADM also requires reports on a quarterly basis (quantitative) and a number of case studies (qualitative) over the course of the programme. The Monitoring Committee for the LURD operational programme monitors the programme at national level.

### 3.4. External evaluation of the action
By ADM and also the external evaluation of the entire programme, regular reports to the Monitoring Committee on the preventive measures undertaken.

## IV. Resources

### 4.1. Human resources used
At local level, each partnership company has an education cordinator who works with teachers and other providers.

### 4.2. Organisational and technical means used
These are project/action specific.

### 4.3. Financial data
Estimate of the cost of the action:
* Overall
  Programme budget IRP 104.7 million (1994-99). IRP 10.5 million is reserved for preventive measures in education. About IRP 20 million is applied overall to education measures.

## V. Innovative features of the action
The Education measure in this programme is one of five measures (Enterprise Creation and Development/Infrastructural & Environmental Action/Community Development/Services to the Unemployed/Education (1. Preventive measures 2. Complementary Education & Training) which together form the basis for local development plans of an integrated nature. The particularly innovative features of the education measure are that actions at primary level are funded and that local priority actions may be funded.

## VI. Comments
Area partnership companies (and other funded groups) are independent companies funded and supported by ADM Ltd in implementing programmes which address locally identified priorities in relation to disadvantage and social exclusion. Typical educational actions would include early childhood care and education programmes involving parents and including training for providers. Interventions at primary and secondary level, e.g. after-school study and other supports, transition programmes primary to secondary, and secondary to third level, learning and psychological support schemes.

## I. Brief description of the action

### 1.1. Name of the project
Community based guidance assistance.

### 1.2. Organisation undertaking the action
National centre for guidance in education — project promoter.

### 1.3. Address
189 Parnell Street.
City: Dublin 1. Country: Ireland.
Tel: (353-1) 873 14 11. Fax: (353-1) 873 13 16.
E-mail: john.mccarthy@leargas.team400.ie
Contact: John Mc Carthy.

### 1.4. Brief description of the action
Training significant persons in the lives of young people at risk in guidance skills so that they can help these young people to integrate into the formal system.

## II. Approach and content

### 2.1. Context, motivation and origin of the initiative
Social and economic exclusion, inability of the formal guidance providers to reach the target group. Use of the existing social relationships of significant persons in the lives of these young people.

### 2.2. Target group (socially excluded youth, long-term unemployed, etc.; give ages and details of the populations concerned; their status)
Social and economic dropouts, aged 12 to 24, poor or non-existent educational qualifications.

### 2.3. Socio-educational approach
Development and delivery of a training programme in non-formal guidance for significant persons, mainly volunteers within the communities in which the target groups live.

### 2.4. Scheduling and length of the action
Two years: 1996 to 1997 needs analysis, design of training, training, implementation, evaluation. One year: dissemination (1998).

### 2.5. Is your action/project in any way part of/supported by a national scheme or legislation, which aims to combat social exclusion?
In Ireland the projects are linked to the development of local responses to long-term unemployment and presentation — part of a national initiative.

## III. Partnerships and means used

### 3.1. Name, status and role of the main partner
National centre for guidance in education Ireland — promoter.

### 3.2. Other partners
Careers Europe, Bradford UK; LDC, Netherlands; CEFOC/UNINOVA, Almada, Lisbon, Portugal.

### 3.3. Monitoring and ongoing evaluation
Formative mainly. Use of external consultant throughout. An assessment at the end of training.

### 3.4. External evaluation of the action

External consultant present at transnational project management meetings and training seminars and on-site evaluation.

## IV. Resources

### 4.1. Human resources used

University personnel, local experts, national experts in guidance, volunteers from communities where target group resides.

### 4.2. Organisational and technical means used

Experiential, participative, negotiated learning.

### 4.3. Financial data

Estimate of the cost of the action:
- Overall: ECU 161 000 approximately. 1995-97: four partners.

## V. Innovative features of the action

1. Developing new strategies for guidance provision to reach the target group.
2. Reconstruction of professional guidance to share skills with community workers and volunteers.
3. Joint trans-national training in guidance for project management personnel.

## VI. Comments

Current focus on sustainability, replication, and dissemination. A boundary-breaking project, making the formal guidance system more sensitive in its strategy to assist young people at risk.

# I. Brief description of the action

### 1.1. Name of the project
YouthReach (Bray and North Wicklow).

### 1.2. Organisation undertaking the action
Co. Wicklow Vocational Education Committee.

### 1.3. Address
Sunbeam House, Vevay Road.
City: Bray, Co. Wicklow. Country: Ireland.
Tel.: (353-1) 286 95 98. Fax: (353-1) 286 96 71.
Contact: A. Burgess.

### 1.4. Brief description of the action
1. Pre-vocational training and general education for early school leavers between the ages of 15 and 18.
2. Training and education for young lone parents.

# II. Approach and content

### 2.1. Context motivation and origin of the initiative
The aim of the YouthReach programme is to give young early school-leavers the skills and understanding to enter the adult world of work or to further education or training.

### 2.2. Target group (socially excluded youth, long-term unemployed, etc.; give ages and details of the populations concerned; their status)
Socially excluded youth — 15 to 18 years old.

### 2.3. Socio-educational approach
Learner centred experiential approach.

### 2.4. Scheduling and length of the action
Participants may attend the YouthReach programme for the duration of two phases — Foundation and Progression. Only Foundation is delivered at the Bray YouthReach centre.

### 2.5. Is your action/project in any way part of/supported by a national scheme or legislation that aims to combat social exclusion?
The Bray YouthReach project is part of the Irish national provision for early school-leavers under a social guarantee that aims to combat social exclusion. Approximately 2 500 young people attend YouthReach centres.

# III. Partnerships and means used

### 3.1. Name, status and role of the main partner
Irish Department of Education and the European Social Fund.

### 3.2. Other partners
Department of Enterprise and Employment (FAS) and vocational Education Committees with ESF.

### 3.3. Monitoring and ongoing evaluation
The Bray YouthReach Centre reports to a vocational education committee Board of Management who submits annual reports and returns to the Department of Education.

**3.4.** **External evaluation of the action**

European Social Fund Evaluation Unit based in Ireland.

## IV.      Resources

**4.1.** **Human resources used**

Trainers/instructors and teachers.

**4.2.** **Organisational and technical means used**

Bray YouthReach Centre has purpose-built training rooms for woodwork, engineering, catering, computers, general education and hair care. It also provides a creche for the children and infants of its participants.

**4.3.** **Financial data**

## V.      Innovative features of the action

1. Compensatory basic education and training for socially disadvantaged early school leavers.
2. Programme of part-time education and training for young lone parents

## VI.      Comments

# I. Brief description of the action

### 1.1. Name of the project
Early School Leaver Measures.

### 1.2. Organisation undertaking the action
FAS.
Training and Employment Authority.

### 1.3. Address
FAS Training Centre, Industrial Park.
City: Waterford. Country: Ireland.
Tel: 051-301 529. Fax: 051-301 530.
E-mail: o.clancy@indigo.ie
Contact: Angela Lambkin.

### 1.4. Brief description of the action
Regional management of community training workshops, progression measure and training programmes for young people.

# II. Approach and content

### 2.1. Context, motivation and origin of the initiative
National programme.

### 2.2. Target group (socially excluded youth, long-term unemployed, etc.; give ages and details of the populations concerned; their status)
Socially excluded youth.
Long-term unemployed.
Early school leavers.

### 2.3. Socio-educational approach
Finding alternative training options.

### 2.4. Scheduling and length of the action
Ongoing.

### 2.5. Is your action/project in any way part of/supported by a national scheme or legislation that aims to combat social exclusion?
n/a.

# III. Partnerships and means used

### 3.1. Name, status and role of the main partner
n/a

### 3.2. Other partners

### 3.3. Monitoring and ongoing evaluation

### 3.4. External evaluation of the action

## IV. Resources

### 4.1. Human resources used
National programme budget.

### 4.2. Organisational and technical means used
Integrated assessment systems.
Guidance and counselling.

### 4.3. Financial data

## V. Innovative features of the action
Developing new progression training programmes to bridge gap between education and main line programmes.

## VI. Comments

# I. Brief description of the action

### 1.1. Name of the project
YouthReach.

### 1.2. Organisation undertaking the action
City of Dublin Vec.

### 1.3. Address
Town Hall, Ballsbridge, Dublin 4.
City: Dublin. Country: Ireland.
Tel.: (353-1) 668 06 14. Fax: (353-1) 668 07 10.
Contact: Briget Moylan.

### 1.4. Brief description of the action
Programme for early school leavers from 15 to 18 years old.

# II. Approach and content

### 2.1. Context, motivation and origin of the initiative
Curriculum, pastoral and statutory.

### 2.2. Target group (socially excluded youth, long-term unemployed, etc.; give ages and details of the populations concerned; their status)
See 1.4.

### 2.3. Socio-educational approach
No qualifications, high level of unemployment.

### 2.4. Scheduling and length of the action
Present phase: 1988-1999.

### 2.5. Is your action/project in any way part of/supported by a national scheme or legislation that aims to combat social exclusion?
Yes — part of social guarantee.

# III. Partnerships and means used

### 3.1. Name, status and role of the main partner
Department of Education.

### 3.2. Other partners
Department of Labour.

### 3.3. Monitoring and ongoing evaluation
NCVA.

### 3.4. External evaluation of the action
National audit.

# IV. Resources

### 4.1. Human resources used
Teachers, guardians, youth workers, law enforcement agencies, etc.

**4.2. Organisational and technical means used**

Centre-based (specialist facilities, e.g. computers).

**4.3. Financial data**

Not available at this time.

## V. Innovative features of the action

Transnational element.
Teaching methods.

## VI. Comments

# I.    Brief description of the action

### 1.1.    Name of the project
YouthReach.

### 1.2.    Organisation undertaking the action
FAS.

### 1.3.    Address
FAS Training Centre.
City: Athlone. Country: Ireland.
Tel: (353-902) 744 81. Fax: (353-902) 75 750.
E-mail: p.con@iol.ie
Contact: Pat Conway.

### 1.4.    Brief description of the action
Identification of early school leavers.
Motivational inputs to identify work goals.
Personal development.
Acquisition of technical skills and related knowledge to pursue goal.
Progression training to achieve goals.


# II.    Approach and content

### 2.1.    Context, motivation and origin of the initiative

### 2.2.    Target group (socially excluded youth, long-term unemployed, etc. give ages and details of the populations concerned; their status)
Persons under 19 years of age who have not completed second-level school.

### 2.3.    Socio-educational approach

### 2.4.    Scheduling and length of the action
Two years.
Year 1: preparatory work;
Year 2: skills training grading is qualification.

### 2.5.    Is your action/project in any way part of/supported by a national scheme or legislation that aims to combat social exclusion?
Yes. YouthReach Programme.


# III.    Partnerships and means used

### 3.1.    Name, status and role of the main partner
FAS, National Training and Employment Authority.

### 3.2.    Other partners
Management committees made up of community groups.
Education.

### 3.3.    Monitoring and ongoing evaluation
1. progression, 2. levels of certification.

### 3.4.    External evaluation of the action
Evaluation report.

# IV. Resources

### 4.1. Human resources used
Three workshops — 10 trainers + 1 advocate.
Training centre — for progression.

### 4.2. Organisational and technical means used

### 4.3. Financial data
Estimate of the cost of the action:
* overall
  IRP 740 000 per annum — operating costs;
* when distinguishing in investment terms: IRP 240 000.

# V. Innovative features of the action

# VI. Comments

## I. Brief description of the action

### 1.1. Name of the project
EU Innovative Programme — Guidance for Young People.

### 1.2. Organisation undertaking the action
FAS National training and employment agency.

### 1.3. Address
27/33 Upper Baggot Street.
City: Dublin 4. Country: Ireland.
Tel.: (353-1) 607 05 92. Fax: (353-1) 607 06 28.
E-mail: O'Connell.Augustine@FAS.IR
Contact person: Guss O'Connell.

### 1.4. Brief description of the action
Training and employing advocates to provide counselling and guidance, using a tailor-made approach, for unqualified early school leavers in rural and urban communities in Ireland.

## II. Approach and content

### 2.1. Context, motivation and origin of the initiative
Early school leavers are under-represented in the workforce and find it extremely difficult to get a secure foothold in the labour market.

### 2.2. Target group (socially excluded youth, long-term unemployed, etc.; give ages and details of the populations concerned; their status)
The 15- to 18-year-old socially excluded youths who leave school early and who experience extremely difficult problems in entering a career.

### 2.3. Socio-educational approach
Guidance and counselling.

### 2.4. Scheduling and length of the action
Two-year period, 1997 to 1998.

### 2.5. Is your action/project in any way part of/supported by a national scheme or legislation that aims to combat social exclusion?
Yes, by YouthReach that is a joint initiative by the Departments of Enterprise, Trade and Employment, and Education and Science, aimed specifically at early school leavers.

## III. Partnerships and means used

### 3.1. Name, status and role of the main partner
Project collaborating with range of partners in Holland, Great Britain and France.

### 3.2. Other partners

### 3.3. Monitoring and ongoing evaluation
Independent action-research evaluation involved together with national and local monitoring committees.

### 3.4. External evaluation of the action
As above.

# IV.     Resources

### 4.1.     Human resources used
Guidance counsellors.

### 4.2.     Organisational and technical means used
In addition to computers for teaching purposes, a special assessment system has been designed and installed.

### 4.3.     Financial data
Estimate of the cost of the action:
*     overall
      ECU 1 million;
*     when distinguishing various financial contributions and making available of technical and human means:
      — in investment terms: 30 %
      — in operating costs: 70 %.

# V.     Innovative features of the action
Provides an independent professional service of career-oriented counsellors and guidance to early school leavers with a range of different interventions, for a number of course providers, for as long as the young person requires it.

# VI.     Comments
The project is in its second year of the two-year pilot. It has been very well received and is making a huge impact.

# Italy

## I. Brief description of the action

### 1.1. Name of the project
Stratega — Learning strategies against exclusion in multi-cultural environments.

### 1.2. Organisation undertaking the action
*Associazione arces.*

### 1.3. Address
Via Lombardia 6 90144.
City: Palermo. Country: Italy.
Tel: (39- 91) 34 66 29. Fax: (39- 91) 34 63 77.
E. Mail: arces@mbox.infcom.it
Contact: Alessandra La Marca.

### 1.4. Brief description of the action
This project aims to combat the exclusion of disadvantaged and migrant youth through: the development of innovative tools and methodologies for the training of trainers in the prevention of school failure and dropping-out; the adoption of cognitive, meta-cognitive and motivational strategies in training; the exchange of good practice examples in this field; the design of training paths, strategies, guides, software and multimedia for the training of trainers/teachers/cultural mediators/human resources officers and the involvement of the families of disadvantaged youth.

## II. Approach and content

### 2.1. Context, motivation and origin of the initiative
One of the problems of the modern world is the exclusion of a large part of the population from the 'modern professional culture' which guarantees the entrance and permanence in the job market. Modern and future Europe needs a flexible work force with an adequate professional culture, able to learn new information and to insert themselves into a strong educational background, made up of competence and knowledge, as new and multi-disciplinary as possible; i.e. a renewed mentality leading to the need for continuous training towards life-long learning. The Stratega project is aimed at fighting against two different exclusions: that of disadvantaged groups and that of migrants. In particular it wants to meet their need of integration into the training and educational system, their need of the necessary, basic skills to find a job.

### 2.2. Target group (socially excluded youth, long-term unemployed, etc.; give ages and details of the populations concerned; their status)
Disadvantaged young people at risk of dropping-out or outside the educational and training system.

Migrants' children at risk of dropping-out or outside the educational and training system. These two groups have no basic skills to help them to integrate into the society and the work world.

2.3. **Socio-educational approach**

Through the exchange of experience and good practice in the field of the support and remedial training of disadvantaged youth and of the training of their trainers we will: Strengthen motivation towards learning and the 'learn to learn' skill of the students of disadvantaged areas; strengthen their basic competence (especially language and logical-mathematical skills); develop their social attitudes and integration into the training system; provide them with the necessary professional skills; enable migrants' children to obtain, through training, the professional skills and basic abilities (especially linguistic) necessary to enter the job market; let a system recognising migrants' previous competence come out and be structured.

This could help migrants to use the skills and competence obtained in their own countries, also in other European countries, so that they won't be forced to accept 'low competence jobs' any more; train teachers of the first years of professional schools and trainers of the training courses in order to let them use didactic and educational strategies for remedial teaching towards young people at risk, who either don't react to the usual strategies or don't have the learning strategies necessary to succeed in 'school work'; train the abovementioned trainers/teachers so that they are able to self-create strategies and methodologies to develop, in disadvantaged youth, the necessary competence for the new professional requirements (analyses and syntheses skills, group-working, problem-solving, self-learning, etc.); provide teachers/trainers with the necessary competence to stimulate students' interest in learning and auto-motivation; involve the families of these young people at risk, so that they can pursue the same aims as the training system, by making their children used to change, responsibility, acceptance and adaptability to what is new; provide mentors, cultural mediators and human resources officers with the cultural and pedagogic-didactic tools necessary to support teachers/trainers, so that they can 'translate' the new methodologies and good practices in their everyday educational work.

2.4. **Scheduling and length of the action**

The action will be carried out for two years and is divided into eight main stages:
1. Implementation of an in-depth study on the features and reasons for school failure and dropout; on the prevention and remedial teaching strategies; on cognitive, meta-cognitive and motivational strategies; on the possibility of establishing a dialogue among the different cultural identities while saving their differences.
2. Collection of good practice examples in the support of disadvantaged youth and their return to school, and of the European competence on their insertion into the training system; joint research in the partner countries on the situation of disadvantaged and migrant young people with the comparison of some common features.
3. Design of tools for secondary education teachers (professional schools) and trainers of training courses as to the cognitive, meta-cognitive and motivational strategies.
4. Design of training paths for trainers, human resources officers in the inter-cultural field, mentors and intercultural assistants (mediators) who could assist teachers also through the promotion of new strategies to be eventually adapted to the teachers' needs.
5. Design of strategies and tools aimed at involving the families of young people at risk and young migrants in initial training, or who are unable to enter it, in order to reduce the gap between family and school.
6. Design and creation of guides, software and multimedia, didactic modules for the training of the target groups.
7. Quality tests in order to verify their effectiveness, with the aid of experts.
8. Creation of a joint database of experiences for the exchange of good practices.

2.5. **Is your action/project in any way part of/supported by a national scheme or legislation that aims to combat social exclusion?**

No.

## III. Partnership and means used

### 3.1. Name, status and role of the main partner

*Université de Mons-Hainaut* (Belgium), public organisation: Prof. Christian Depover, *Unité de Technologie de l'Education*; they are experts in open and distance learning and will design and create the multimedia products.

*Pedagogische Hochschule Freiburg* (Germany), public organisation: Prof. Norbert Boteram, Pedagogy Chair, expert on schooling and linguistic education of migrants' children. They have carried out many surveys on the relation among language, identity and immigration. They also coordinate an Erasmus project about intercultural pedagogy. They will design the intercultural, cognitive and meta-cognitive strategies.

### 3.2. Other partners

*Università degli Studi di Palermo:* General Didactic Chair, Prof. Giuseppe Zanniello: competence on the realisation of guides, software and multimedia; cooperation in the dropout problem; participation in different European projects (for example: School orientates School' sub-projects 14.2 and 14.3); coordinator of an Erasmus project;

*Associazione Pedagogica Italiana (AS.PE.I.):* one of the national groupings of pedagogists; its participation guarantees, through the 'AS.PE.I Newsletter', the national meetings and activities which its sections organise, the dissemination at national level of the project outcomes, in particular to all pedagogists and bodies concerned with pedagogical themes.

*Association Européenne des Enseignants* (AEDE): it strengthens the European dimension of the project and its multiplier effect; created in 1956, with over 30 000 members, it involves teachers interested in the introduction of a European dimension in education; it cooperates with other trainers, school heads associations and networks for the research and development in the education field (ATEE, ESHA, Concorde); it publishes the magazine 'Context' through which we will spread the outcome of the project.

### 3.3. Monitoring and ongoing evaluation

For each stage we will determine the aims to be pursued, in progress and for the final stage. Results and products will be evaluated according to their correspondence to some parameters, useful to determine how the estimated aims have been reached (innovation, effectiveness, feasibility, transferability, multiplier effect, number of people from the direct target groups involved, acquisition of new skills, and so on).

We will also analyse the relation between results and resources used to obtain them.

All partners will pay attention to the methodological choice of tools and products and measure them up to the final aims, the financial resources exploited, and the final reactions of the direct beneficiaries.

The continuous monitoring system of the management group will also evaluate the effectiveness of the partnership (aims of the transnational cooperation/final results).

### 3.4. External evaluation of the action

We would like to consider an eventual external assessment activity, in order to increase coherency and validity of the process as well as the project impact.

## IV. Resources

### 4.1. Human resources used (teachers, guardians)

Experts in the education and training of disadvantaged youth, teachers, trainers, mentors, cultural mediators, human resources officers.

### 4.2. Organisational and technical means used (facilities, new technology, etc.)

Internet connection; video-conference; software and multimedia.

**4.3.** **Financial data**

The estimated cost of the action is: ECU 265 089.

Each partner will give a personal contribution to the project.

Most expenses will cover the personnel costs and the design and creation of tools and methodologies.

## V. Innovative features of the action

The innovation of this action relates to the new approach, which will be made in the design and realisation of products and methodologies.

The educational methodology used will be based on the awareness that a deep intellectual training and authentic job training, through the enhancement of the value of each beneficiary, can make intercultural exchange among young people easier and help them to enter the production world.

## VI. Comments

This project also aims to stimulate follow-up activities, cooperation among different education and training bodies and to raise the awareness of the target group problems especially in the public institutions sector. For this reason we have requested and obtained an expression of interest by many local institutions operating in this field.

# I. Brief description of the action

### 1.1. Name of the project
JANUS Regional project for social integration and youth employment in the European Union.

### 1.2. Organisation undertaking the action
Emilia-Romagna region — *Assessorato Formazione Lavoro Università Immigrazione* — Training Policy Planning Department.

### 1.3. Address
Assessorato Formazione Lavoro Università Immigrazione — Viale Aldo Moro, 38.
Town: 40127 Bologna. Country: Italy.
Tel. (39-51) 28 38 80. Fax: (39-51) 28 39 36.
E-mail: progr-fp@regione.emilia-romagna.it
Contact: Marie-Françoise Delatour.

### 1.4. Brief description of the action:
Development and testing of a new initial training model for young people with no qualifications, for distribution throughout the region.
Training courses geared to overcoming school failure and remotivating students to obtain qualifications and find jobs.

# II. Approach and content

### 2.1. Context, motivation and origin of the initiative
Need to find a different approach from the traditional class-based organisation and to adapt the general organisation of training centres to set up courses that are motivating for young people excluded from normal schooling.

### 2.2. Target group
Young people aged between 15 and 19 who drop out of, or are expelled from, secondary school.

### 2.3. Socio-educational approach
Stimulating individual motivation to learn.
Guidance throughout training.
Use of new educational technologies.
Support services.

### 2.4. Scheduling and length of the action
This is an integrated project that commenced in 1996 with surveys in conjunction with applied research, and is scheduled to end in December 1998. It is of interest to several training centres in Emilia-Romagna.

### 2.5. Is your action/project in any way part of/supported by a national scheme or legislation that aims to combat social exclusion?
Employ — Youthstart programme.

# III. Partnerships and means used

### 3.1. Name, status and role of the main partner
The Emilia-Romagna Regional Authority is responsible for initial vocational training for young people.

### 3.2. Other partners

Nine public and private vocational training organisations, the University of Bologna/Pedagogical and Social Sciences.

### 3.3. Monitoring and ongoing evaluation

The project has an advisory committee responsible for policy and monitoring, which holds meetings on a regular basis and evaluates the reports from the project heads and the overall project director.

### 3.4. External evaluation of the action

Points for consideration, the working methods and instruments developed, and the interim results are presented and discussed regularly (twice a year) at open seminars.

## IV. Resources

### 4.1. Human resources used

40 trainers, 10 training centre directors, 12 vocational guidance counsellors, 25 company-based mentors, 10 experts (university, consultants and managers of professional organisations).

### 4.2. Organisational and technical means used

Fifteen training centres for the testing, production and use of educational hypertexts and CD-ROMs: use of distance learning for training of instructors (multimedia resources centre).

### 4.3. Financial data

Estimated cost of the project:
* Total: ECU 1 709 845;
  broken down by financial input and technical and human resources:
  — investment 10 %
  — operating costs 90 %.

## V. Innovative features of the action

This is a strategic project forming part of the reform of the initial training system in Emilia-Romagna, which is one element of the national plan to review school education. The project enables each element of the planned new model to be tested separately before implementing it.

## VI. Comments

The project, which was set up in 1996 without any particular ambitions as far as the reorganisation of training centres was concerned, has grown in importance as it has developed, and with the commencement of discussion of the results of the surveys and research has been attracting the attention of all the public decision-makers and associations concerned with the training of young people in the Region.

# I. Brief description of the action

### 1.1. Name of the project
*Trasparenza delle certificazioni.*

### 1.2. Organisation undertaking the action
*Consorzio Istituti Emilia Romagna.*

### 1.3. Address
IPSSSCT 'Don Zeffirino Jodi' — Via della Canalina, 21/1.
City: Reggio Emilia. Country: Italia.
Tel.: (39-522) 32 57 11. Fax: (39-522) 29 42 33.
E-mail: jodi@re.nettuno.it
Contact: Ettore Piazza.

### 1.4. Brief description of the action
Definition of methodologies of certification, in order to assure transparency.
Define needed changes in the ways student' skills are assessed in final examinations.
Providing students with trans-national qualifications.
Obtaining qualifications by attending modules in different countries.

# II. Approach and content

### 2.1. Context, motivation and origin of the initiative
For the students participating in the project the partnership pursues the opportunity of attending learning modules abroad so they can join the experience acquired in a foreign country to the continuing of their life. For the teachers involved the partnership pursues acquisition of knowledge of various systems regarding the professional profile they will be dealing with in order to obtain transparency in the certifications of various professional figures.

### 2.2. Target group (socially excluded youth, long-term unemployed, etc.; give ages and details of the populations concerned; their status)
Students in initial vocational training.
Trainers under 55 years.
Students with diplomas.

### 2.3. Socio-educational approach
The development of a European education for a transparency in the certifications achieved, through the definition of common teaching modules which will enable students and trainers to work and to continue their training in various European countries. We aim to get easier mobility for workers inside Europe.

### 2.4. Scheduling and length of the action
Preliminary work at national level.
Comparative analysis of the methods of evaluation and qualification adopted in the countries involved in the partnership.
Exchange of ideas about the different training levels.
Analysis of formal and informal systems of certification.
Analysis of the systems of acknowledgement of qualifications.
Identification of common criteria of certification.
Experimental elaboration of common certificates.
Experimentation in different working contexts.

**2.5.** **Is your action/project in any way part of/supported by a national scheme or legislation that aims to combat social exclusion?**

## III. Partnerships and means used

**3.1.** **Name, status and role of the main partner**
BIFHE Belfast Institute (UK) — Social Services.
IFW Irish Federation of Cooperatives (IRL) — business issues.
Lycée Hotelier, Dinard (F) — tourism projects.
CNC Zentrum, Hamburg (D).

**3.2.** **Other partners**
Senajoki Politecnic (FIN).
Lycée Gambetta Bourgoin Jallieu.
Jewel College Edinburgh (UK).

**3.3.** **Monitoring and ongoing evaluation**
Improvement of linguistic skills with reference to the use of the English language. Improving the knowledge of the specific terminology relevant to the various professional areas.

**3.4.** **External evaluation of the action**
The managers of the project will define and collect the results for evaluation.

## IV. Resources

**4.1.** **Human resources used**
Trainers, headmasters, administrative personnel, tutors, language training experts.

**4.2.** **Organisational and technical means used**
We have worked in national and international meeting with the support of telephone, fax, and e-mail.

**4.3.** **Financial data**
Estimate of the cost of the action:
- overall: general costs: ECU 51 000; travel and subsistence costs: ECU 180 000; other costs: ECU 3 500.

## V. Innovative features of the action
The project will make changes in the methodologies of certification, in the assessment systems, in the interaction between employer and employee.

## VI. Comments

# Luxembourg

## I. Brief description of the action

**1.1. Name of project**

'Integrated pathways to integration for the young unemployed'.

**1.2. Organisation undertaking the action:**

*Action Sociale Pour Jeunes* (non-profit-making association).

**1.3. Address**

ASJ — 1 rue du Moulin, L-3857 Schifflange.
Tel. (352) 53 04 45-0.
Fax: (352) 53 04 45-40
Contact: Romain Biever.

**1.4. Brief description of the action**

Our main aim is to combat unemployment and exclusion among disadvantaged young job seekers. To do this, we are implementing global pathways to integration, bringing together research, training and placement, enabling young people to acquire social and vocational skills.

## II. Approach and content

**2.1. Context, motivation and origin of the initiative**

Rising unemployment in Luxembourg and the lack of training systems for young adults have lead ASJ to design new training models in line with new socioeconomic developments.

**2.2. Target groups**

Young adults aged between 16 and 30 who have left school with no certificates or qualifications and, for the most part, also have various social problems (family, housing, the law, money, health, drugs, etc.). They are registered with the employment administration as job seekers.

**2.3. Socio-educational approach**

Training is based on 'learning by doing'. This method is relevant to our target group as most young adults lack a sufficient theoretical basis and cannot relate to traditional teaching.

**2.4. Scheduling and length of the action**

The training lasts up to two years, beginning with a four-month practical phase working on various sites. At the end of this stage, participants will be allocated, in accordance with their skills and preferences, to a training site (*'chantier école'*) where they will receive eight months of general training. During the following 12 months, they will receive specialised training to acquire marketable skills.

### 2.5. National/European support for contact against exclusion

*At national level:*

Partnership with the highways department (*Administration des Ponts et Chaussées*), the Chamber of Craft Trades, and the Ministries of the Environment, Labour and Employment.

*At European level:*

ESF Article 6 grants for the CFM and various programmes (FORCE, Leonardo, etc.).

## III. Partnerships and means used

### 3.1. Role of the main partner

The *Ponts et Chaussées* is both our main customer with regard to infrastructure work and an effective partner providing human and logistical resources for our training courses.

### 3.2. Other partners

- The Chamber of Craft Trades is a very important partner, as it has officially recognised ASJ as a training body following three years' cooperation and guidance.
- Europe, thanks to the financial support provided in the CFM pilot project (ESF Article 6).
- Local authorities and the OGB-L; *'Objectif Plein Emploi'*.
- Associations
- Private undertakings (*'Réseau Patron'*).

### 3.3. Monitoring and ongoing evaluation

In parallel with the training programme and various local socio-economic development projects, we have introduced tools for monitoring and assessing participants in terms of both social and technical skills.

### 3.4. External evaluation of the action

Regular assessment by external financial partners (the State, Europe) in the context of the various projects.

## IV. Resources

### 4.1. Human resources used

A multidisciplinary team bringing together technical and general supervisory staff, a psychologist, administrative and accounting staff, management and multimedia graphic artists.

### 4.2. Organisational and technical means used

A number of work sites:
— one building in Luxembourg/Eich provided by the State;
— one renovated former mill in Schifflange, administered by us and belonging to the State;
— one training centre in Fentange, former factory premises rented by us and with installation work currently underway;
— Highways Department premises in Bertrange housing the training centre *'Métiers Traditionnels'* (traditional crafts).

### 4.3. Financial data

Annual budget for the measure: ECU 2.5 million, over 60 % of which is covered by turnover, with 15 % in public funds from the Luxembourg State and 12 % in European funding.

## V. Innovative features of the action in the local context

The aim of ASJ is not to organise production sites but rather to develop a form of cooperation with public and private undertakings interested in our package:

— training courses;
— innovative teaching tools;
— research and development/activity sectors providing jobs and to promote this form of work among the national authorities

## VI. Comments

Having in the past used the 'responsible citizens' (non-profit-making association) and 'local development' approaches, we have been able to prepare a favourable political and socio-economic environment for any approaches aimed at introducing what is now known as the 'third sector'.

## I. Brief description of the action

### 1.1. Name of the project
*Objectif Plein Emploi* ('Objective: a job for everyone').

### 1.2. Organisation undertaking the action
Comité Intercommunal Pour Le Développement (CIDE).

### 1.3. Address
CIDE, 1, rue du Moulin.
City: Schifflange. Country: Luxembourg.
Tel.: (352) 04 45 21. Fax: (352) 04 45 41.
E-mail: charles@asj.lu
Contact: Charles Laplanche.

### 1.4. Brief description of the action
*Objectif Plein Emploi* seeks to address the problem of unemployment through local and regional projects, and to introduce effective local structures to cater for the needs of job seekers.

## II. Approach and content

### 2.1. Context, motivation and origin of the initiative
The region concerned is in the south of Luxembourg and the action is undertaken jointly by Luxembourg's main trade union, the OGBL (*Confédération syndicale indépendante – Luxembourg*) and Action sociale pour jeunes. The essential motivation is to get job seekers back into the employment market.

### 2.2. Target group (socially excluded youth, long-term unemployed, etc.; give ages and details of the populations concerned; their status)
All job seekers irrespective of age, sex or qualifications. Status: registered job seeker.

### 2.3. Socio-educational approach
The approach varies according to the project but is essentially geared to helping unemployed persons to become qualified through practical training and to familiarise them with the new technologies using theoretical training.

### 2.4. Scheduling and length of the action
The action commenced in April 1997 thanks to joint funding under the ESF and the *Fonds pour l'emploi*. No time limit has been set for this action.

### 2.5. Is your action/project in any way part of/supported by a national scheme or legislation that aims to combat social exclusion?
Yes: ESF, *Fonds national pour l'emploi*.

## III. Partnerships and means used

### 3.1. Name, status and role of the main partner
The main partner is the employment department, which is responsible for the recruitment and placement of unemployed persons.

### 3.2. Other partners
Ministry for Education (vocational training department), trade unions, employers and firms, Chamber of Trades.

**3.3.** **Monitoring and ongoing evaluation**

A database will be used to manage the projects, material and human resources, and to monitor the progress of each job seeker.

**3.4.** **External evaluation of the action**

The Ministry will monitor the action for Labour.

The Ministry will monitor the action for Labour and the municipalities concerned.

## IV. Resources

**4.1.** **Human resources used**

10 development agents, 20 trainers and a comprehensive partnership.

**4.2.** **Organisational and technical means used**

Considerable means will be deployed, including the new technologies, and will depend on the specific project.

**4.3.** **Financial data**

Estimate of the cost of the action:

- Overall: LUF 200 million yearly.
- When distinguishing various financial contributions and making available of technical and human means:
  — in investment terms: LUF 50 million.
  — in operating costs: LUF 150 million.

## V. Innovative features of the action in the local context

- All the projects are developed at local level in partnership wish are all the local socio-economic partners.
- Integration of new technology in the local development process.

## VI. Comments

# Portugal

## I. Brief description of the action

### 1.1. Name of the project
*JIVA — Jovens Inserção na Vida Activa.*

### 1.2. Organisation undertaking the action
Centro Social Paroquial Santo Antonio de Campolide.

### 1.3. Address
Rua Dom Carlos de Macarenhas 23 r/c.
City: Lisbon. Country: Portugal.
Tel: (351-1) 386 19 02. Fax: (351-1) –388 29 43.
E-mail: jiva esotérica.pt
Contact: Maria Eugenia Santiago.

### 1.4. Brief description of the action
We develop activities that aim at the personal, cultural and social qualifications of the project's subjects and actors, by the (re)cognition of their own competencies and abilities, translated on a first stage and fundamentally to the acquisition of knowledge — to know, to know how to be, to know how to do in order to achieve their professional skills, and the consequent integration on the labour market.

## II. Approach and content

### 2.1. Context, motivation and origin of the initiative
The characteristics of the region where we are working: drugs dependencies, alcoholism, robbers, low education profile, unemployment. This motivated us to develop social help and care for the most marginalised families in the community.

### 2.2. Target group (socially excluded youth, long-term unemployed, etc.; give ages and details of the populations concerned; their status)
Among 90 youths living in socially excluded places without motivation to attend school, and big problems in the integration into the labour market because they have a very low level of personal and professional qualifications

### 2.3. Socio-educational approach
Through a development-integrated model, we promote the individual, collective and political empowerment of people in the community.

### 2.4. Scheduling and length of the action
During the entire project.

**2.5.** **Is your action/project in any way part of/supported by a national scheme or legislation that aims to combat social exclusion?**


**III.** **Partnerships and means used**

**3.1.** **Name, status and role of the main partner**
GIP and IMBSE — Germany.
Finnish Association for Mental Health — Finland.

**3.2.** **Other partners**
Youth Action — Northern Ireland.

**3.3.** **Monitoring and ongoing evaluation**

**3.4.** **External evaluation of the action**


**IV.** **Resources**

**4.1.** **Human resources used**
Social workers.

**4.2.** **Organisational and technical means used**
Multimedia centre, Internet.

**4.3.** **Financial data**


**V.** **Innovative features of the action**


**VI.** **Comments**
The target group conditions and involvment induce us to establish as first big aims the motivation of youth to acquire the knowedge and the capacity to integrate themselves and/or to stay in the educational training or employment system.

# I. Brief description of the action

### 1.1. Name of the project
*Pre Aprendizagem.*

### 1.2. Organisation undertaking the action
*Santa Casa da Misericordia da Sintra.*

### 1.3. Address
Rua da Pendoa, nº 17, 2170 Sintra.
City: Sintra. Country: Portugal.
Tel.: (351-1) 924 15 46. Fax: (351-1) 924 10 92.
Contact: Maria Belem Leitao.

### 1.4. Brief description of the action
The action had devoted to youth in exclusion situation, without school learning, had as objective offer them this school learning and a professional pre-qualification, had developed to seven dissimilar professional areas, surpasses the component of formulation, developed a programme of social and professional insertion

# II. Approach and content

### 2.1. Context, motivation and origin of the initiative
Context — High percentage of youth at risk of social exclusion in Sintra Council, solicitation of family and schools, motivation community insertion of *Santa Casa da Misericordia de Sintra.*
Origin of the Initiative — *Santa Casa da Misericordia de Sintra* and employment centre of Amadora.

### 2.2. Target group (socially excluded youth, long-term unemployed, etc.; give ages and details of the populations concerned; their status)
Socially excluded youth, between 14 and 18 years, without school learning and with inadequate social conducts.

### 2.3. Socio-educational approach
Psycho-social attendance of youth.
Dynamics of groups — two hours per week.
Social attendance of family.
Support to professional integration of youth.

### 2.4. Scheduling and length of the action
The training was of one year — seven hours a day.
The social programme — three years.

### 2.5. Is your action/project in any way part of/supported by a national scheme or legislation that aims to combat social exclusion?
No.

# III. Partnerships and means used

### 3.1. Name, status and role of the main partner
Employment centre of Amadora, CRSSLVT. Sub-regional service of Sintra, State Department of Social Security and Employment.

**3.2.** **Other partners**
Monte-Abraao Church of Queluz.
Cruz Vermelha Portuguesa — Queluz Nucleus.

**3.3.** **Monitoring and ongoing evaluation**
Monthly evaluation, by technical team and educators, of individual situation of each youth.

**3.4.** **External evaluation of the action**
Formally, only the evaluation of Santa Casa and the result of youth insertion (85 youths), 69 had social and professional insertion, from these, 20 come back for night school.

## IV. Resources

**4.1.** **Human resources used**
Social workers (5), teachers (30), pedagogic adviser (1), social adviser (1), administrator (1), cook (1), Psychiatrist (1).

**4.2.** **Organisational and technical means used**
The formation (education) was based on the method 'Learning by Doing', and the continuation of youth in the social programme until to them framing into community structure.

**4.3.** **Financial data**

## V. Innovative features of the action
To come operational the action, where the final objective is the insertion and not only the formation, because the social programme as much importance as the formation

## VI. Comments

# I. Brief description of the action

### 1.1. Name of the project
Professional insertion of young fishermen.

### 1.2. Organisation undertaking the action
Forpescas — Fisheries Vocational Training Centre.

### 1.3. Address
Av. Brasília, Pedroixos 1400.
City: Lisbon. Country: Portugal.
Tel: (351-1) 301 76 70. Fax: (351-1) 301 64 82.
E-mail: forpescas@mail.telepac.pt
Contact: Manuela Correia Lopes.

### 1.4. Brief description of the action
Professional qualification (Level 1) and schooling equivalence to 4th minimum level required for young people with academic difficulties.

# II. Approach and content

### 2.1. Context, motivation and origin of the initiative
This training is part of a national training system. Since fisheries populations show low levels of schooling and the rate of young school-leavers is high, this type of training is particularly important.

### 2.2. Target group (socially excluded youth, long-term unemployed, etc.; give ages and details of the populations concerned; their status)
Young people aged between 14 and 21 years who have not completed their schooling cycle.

### 2.3. Socio-educational approach
The training course, with a total duration of one year, provides basic training units such as mathematics, foreign languages and environmental sciences, which give schooling equivalence.

### 2.4. Scheduling and length of the action
The course has 1 500 training hours (35 hours/week) during daytime.

### 2.5. Is your action/project in any way part of/supported by a national scheme or legislation that aims to combat social exclusion?
Yes, the project is supported by Governmental Decree 279/91 of April 1991.

# III. Partnerships and means used

### 3.1. Name, status and role of the main partner

### 3.2. Other partners

### 3.3. Monitoring and ongoing evaluation
Trainees are evaluated during the course, and at the end a professional certificate is given to those who achieve the necessary knowledge and course goals.

### 3.4. External evaluation of the action

## IV.    Resources

### 4.1.    Human resources used
Internal and external trainers training course. Coordinator and training on-the-job evaluator.

### 4.2.    Organisational and technical means used
This training course takes place on Forpescas training facilities involving nine training centres.

### 4.3.    Financial data
Estimate of the cost of the action: ECU 100 000 (trainees receive financial compensation).

## V.    Innovative features of the action
To contribute to the social and professional insertion of young people, providing the possibility of increasing academic qualifications through a vocational training course.

## VI.    Comments

# I. Brief description of the action

### 1.1. Name of the project
Structuring and organisation of the Seixal (Portugal) second chance project.

### 1.2. Organisation undertaking the action
*CDR — Cooperaçâo e desenvolvimento regional.*

### 1.3. Address
CDR.
City: Setúbal. Country: Portugal.
Tel.: (351-65) 53 45 50. Fax: (351- 65) 53 47 20.
E-mail: cdr@cdr.pt
Contact: Celia Pereira.

### 1.4. Brief description of the action
Adjustments, tentative approaches and transition pathways, the objective being to implement a change with a view to a different network of social integration which is more amenable to social subcultures.

# II. Approach and content

### 2.1. Context, motivation and origin of the initiative

### 2.2. Target group (socially excluded youth, long-term unemployed, etc.; give ages and details of the populations concerned; their status)
Young people under legal age, living in socially precarious areas, who have a stormy background and face certain risks.

### 2.3. Socio-educational approach
Multidimensional educational and training action including psycho-pedagogical principles, standards, a context of socialisation and behaviour, organisation of areas, communication and making use of free time.

### 2.4. Scheduling and length of the action

### 2.5. Is your action/project in any way part of/supported by a national scheme or legislation that aims to combat social exclusion?

# III. Partnerships and means used

### 3.1. Name, status and role of the main partner

### 3.2. Other partners
Ministry of Labour, Ministry of Education, firms, VT centre, Sta. Casa da Misericordia, Bento Jesus Caraça school.

### 3.3. Monitoring and ongoing evaluation

### 3.4. External evaluation of the action

## IV.    Resources

### 4.1.    Human resources used
Ministry of Education, company staff, VT centre staff.

### 4.2.    Organisational and technical means used
Ministry of Science and Technology; Microsoft Internet Web Site.

### 4.3.    Financial data

## V.    Innovative features of the action

## VI.    Comments

# I. Brief description of the action

### 1.1. Name of the project
Transitar Project.

### 1.2. Organisation undertaking the action
RUMO.

### 1.3. Address
City: 2860 Moita. Country: Portugal.
Tel: (351-1) 238 13 08. Fax: (351-1) 236 32 86.
E-mail: rumopen@mail.telepac.pt
Contact: Augusto Sousa.

### 1.4. Brief description of the action
Link the basic education with on-the-job training and employment.
Vocational guidance in real context (companies and community).
Individual plans for each person.
Involvement of employers, parents, teachers, other professionals.

# II. Approach and content

### 2.1. Context, motivation and origin of the initiative
Lack of a good process of transition from school (basic education) to social and work inclusion.
Fight against the early leaving of school.

### 2.2. Target group (socially excluded youth, long-term unemployed, etc.; give ages and details of the populations concerned; their status)
Socially excluded youth, from 15 years of age.

### 2.3. Socio-educational approach
Local network between regular schools, professional schools, companies, and employment centres.
Systemic approach. Individual training places and programmes.

### 2.4. Scheduling and length of the action

### 2.5. Is your action/project in any way part of/supported by a national scheme or legislation that aims to combat social exclusion?
Yes.
New legislation trying to link programmes promoted by educational authorities with vocational training and employment authorities.

# III. Partnerships and means used

### 3.1. Name, status and role of the main partner
Seixal City Council.
Ministry of Education.

### 3.2. Other partners
Employment centres, employers, regular schools.

### 3.3. Monitoring and ongoing evaluation
Each year — interim report.
Continuous — monitoring of each student/trainee, processes and results.

**3.4.** **External evaluation of the action**
To be defined.

## IV.    Resources

**4.1.** **Human resources used**
Teachers, vocational trainers, mentors/tutors.

**4.2.** **Organisational and technical means used**
New technologies, specific facility related to professional school and companies as the main means to develop vocational training.

**4.3.** **Financial data**

## V.    Innovative features of the action

A new approach in order to link clearly the field of education with the field of vocational training and employment and also the active role of community.

## VI.    Comments

# Spain

## I. Brief description of the action

### 1.1. Name of the project
*Escuelas Taller de Gijón* (Workshop Schools of Gijón).

### 1.2. Organisation undertaking the action
*Ayuntamiento de Gijón* (City Council of Gijón).

### 1.3. Address
Casa de Rosario Acuña. Camino de los Arces, s/n.
City: Gijón. Country: Spain.
Tel.: (34) 985 13 25 65.
E-mail: etaller@netcom.es
Contact: Rosa Iglesias.

### 1.4. Brief description of the action
The Escuelas Taller (workshop schools) programme is part of the Government's employment policy for the youth. It aims at the creation of jobs through a training programme accompanied by professional practice in activities related to the rehabilitation of the cultural, natural, urban and industrial heritage.

## II. Approach and content

### 2.1. Context, motivation and origin of the initiative
The programme started experimentally in 1985 under the direction of the *Instituto Nacional de Empleo* (National Employment Agency), then regulated by legislation from the Ministry of Labour and Social Security.

### 2.2. Target group (socially excluded youth, long-term unemployed, etc.; give ages and details of the populations concerned; their status)
Unemployed young people, having a degree or not, ranging from the school-leaving age (16 years) to under 25 years old. Coming from various social positions.

### 2.3. Socio-educational approach
Social integration and integration in the community through the contribution of real and useful work to the city in which the young live.

### 2.4. Scheduling and length of the action
The length of each workshop school was fixed since 1994 to two years (formerly it was three years). Divided into two stages: (a) occupational training, during six months; (b) professional experience, till the end of the project.

**2.5.** **Is your action/project in any way part of/supported by a national scheme or legislation that aims to combat social exclusion?**

Not expressly, though there are many handicapped, former drug addicts, or school dropouts included in the programme Escuelas Taller of Gijón.

## III. Partnerships and means used

**3.1.** **Name, status and role of the main partner**

Instituto *Nacional de Employ*, is the national agency for employment, dependent on the Ministry of Labour and Social Security.

**3.2.** **Other partners**

European Social Fund (through the National Employment Agency) and the City Council of Gijón.

**3.3.** **Monitoring and ongoing evaluation**

These are carried out both by the teachers of the Workshop School and by the local office of the National Employment Agency.

**3.4.** **External evaluation of the action**

## IV. Resources

**4.1.** **Human resources used**

It depends on the project. They usually include primary education teachers, teachers coming from different professional sectors, master builder, headmistress or headmaster, etc.

**4.2.** **Organisational and technical means used**

Depending on the project. They mainly revolve around construction, environment, gardening, woodwork, etc., but also audiovisual communications, restoration, bookbinding, conservation and recuperation of historical archives, computer-assisted cataloguing, etc.

**4.3.** **Financial data**

The Workshop Schools of Gijón budget for 1998 is ESP 265 520 297, of which ESP 213 996 950 are given by the National Employment Agency and ESP 51 523 348 by the City Council of Gijón. Overall, ESP 226 920 103 in investment terms and ESP 38 600 195 in operating costs.

## V. Innovative features of the action

The student-workers are paid a salary while acquiring professional experience.

## VI. Comments

## I.	Brief description of the action

### 1.1.	Name of the project
Social integration of young people with risk of social exclusion.

### 1.2.	Organisation undertaking the action
*Asociación semilla para la integración social del joven.*

### 1.3.	Address
Asociación Semilla (Lourdes Ibañez), C/ Alabierna, 9.
City: Madrid 28021. Country: Spain.
Tel: (34-91) 798 69 55. Fax: (34-91) 798 43 51.
E-mail: semilla@arrakis.es
Contact: Emilio Lazaro Blanco.

### 1.4.	Brief description of the action
A day centre is the first step in Outreach, and social contact, self-esteem and group work is encouraged. Then the students attend professional workshops where they train for a profession. A job club connects them with employment. Also, practice in companies or shops the association owns, provide a first year job opportunity.

## II.	Approach and content

### 2.1.	Context, motivation and origin of the initiative
High level of school dropout in the area south of Madrid, with drugs and violence problems in the schools. High unemployment rates and difficulties accessing the work market.

### 2.2.	Target group (socially excluded youth, long-term unemployed, etc.; give ages and details of the populations concerned; their status)
Students outside the regulated education system.
Familiar difficulties: economic, unstructuration, unemployed parents.
Lack of access to culture and personal growth.
Socially excluded young people who have failed at school. Aged 14 to 21, all of them are unemployed.

### 2.3.	Socio-educational approach
The failure at school is related to family troubles, drugs and economic difficulties. Our approach includes dealing with families, individualised educative processes, small group tutorials and following up and cultural education based on generating subjects, and social project: helping community with some works. Also, training vocational attitudes. We pursue the autonomy and critical insertion in society.

### 2.4.	Scheduling and length of the action
The day centre is attended between two and ten months, depending on each student.
The professional workshops take two years for most of the students, divided in three training modules. Some students need more time for completing.
Completion with practice period near, or close by, or own company for one year.

### 2.5.	Is your action/project in any way part of/supported by a national scheme or legislation that aims to combat social exclusion?
Social warranty programmes of the education and culture ministry of Spain.
Youthstart programme supported by *Comunidad de Madrid* (insol).
Integra programmes supported by *Comunidad de Madrid*.
Participation in different actions of the Youth for Europe programme.
Ministry of Social Affairs.
Private donations.
Madrid town hall.

## III. Partnerships and means used

**3.1. Name, status and role of the main partner**
Comunidad de Madrid: local government.
Role: funding.

**3.2. Other partners**
WAC (England), IFAP (Germany), Dynamo (Belgium), Anima (Portugal),
Subcentro e.i.c. (Italy).

**3.3. Monitoring and ongoing evaluation**
Initial evaluation: family, culture, level at school.
Continual evaluation through tutorial and PEI (individualised educational process).
Trinestral evaluation of both youngster and project.
Self-evaluation.
Follow-up after leaving.s

**3.4. External evaluation of the action**
The organisations that support the project make a periodical evaluation in economic and
pedagogical aspects.
A training of trainers project evaluates pedagogy, psychology and procedures through weekly
meetings with a psycho-educative coordinator.

## IV. Resources

**4.1. Human resources used**
2 employment insertion specialists
8 teachers
2 pedagogues
3 social workers
1 psychologist
1 secretary
1 accountant
1 with financial responsibility
13 workshop trainers
1 street trainer
1 European volunteer
14 volunteers
15 university practising students.

**4.2. Organisational and technical means used**
One workshop of cooking and catering; one workshop of computers; one workshop of textile
design; one parents school; one youth information centre; several computers with connection
to Internet; one school support centre.

**4.3. Financial data**
Estimate of the cost of the action:
* overall
    ESP 120 million a year

## V. Innovative features of the action
- Strong outreach action and normalisation in day centre;
- a job club that links the training with profession;
- social project: works and commitment in community;
- teacher´s training programme, needs-based education system and cooperative inquierty;
- continuity of care from the early stages to employment;
- parents school.

## VI. Comments
We would like to make contact with other European organisations that develop similar work with young people. As well as getting economic resources for developing our initiatives from the European Union.

# I. Brief description of the action

### 1.1. Name of the project
Second Chance School of Bilbao. European pilot project.

### 1.2. Organisation undertaking the action.
Lan Ekintza-Bilbao, S.A., a municipal company of Bilbao.

### 1.3. Address
Uribitarte, 18 — 4° dcha.
City: 48001 Bilbao. Country: Spain.
Tel.: (34-94) 420 53 00. Fax: (34-94) 420 53 13.
E-mail: lan-ekintza@lane.bilbao.net
Contact: Ricardo Barkala Zumelzu.

### 1.4. Brief description of the action:
The action is within the framework of the Second Chance Schools network, European pilot project of the European Community.

Second Chance Schools pilot projects to provide new opportunities through education and training directed at young people who lack both the basic knowledge and the specific competencies to benefit fully from training or to find employment.

The Bilbao Second Chance School attempts to provide a solution to the problems (school failures, unemployment, social exclusion, integration, etc.) of disadvantaged youths from problem areas of Bilbao.

# II. Approach and content

### 2.1. Context, motivation and origin of the initiative
In the Bilbao metropolitan area, declining traditional industries such as steel and shipbuilding. No less than 25.7 % of the active population is unemployed (41 800 in total) of which 70 % for more than a year. Youth unemployment is 57 %. In the population age group 15 to 19, approximately 10 % had no primary school diplomas and by the final year of compulsory education in Bilbao the failure rate is 27 to 30 %.

The initiative attempts to provide a solution to the problems of school failures or dropouts of disadvantaged youths from problematic areas of Bilbao.

### 2.2. Target group (socially excluded youth, long-term unemployed, etc.; give ages and details of the populations concerned; their status)
The target group is 150 young persons over 16 years old. They live in Bilbao la Vieja the old harbour area of Bilbao and Otxarkoaga district, which are characterised by a multitude of urban problems: urban degradation, pollution, unemployment, poverty, prostitution. Typically these young people find themselves with low levels of basic skills, frequently coupled with negative experiences of education. With no prospects of improving their social situation, they risk being caught in an irreversible spiral of marginalisation and exclusion.

### 2.3. Socio-educational approach
— Needs addressed on two basic axes:
    1. personal and social development
    2. development of capabilities required to handle working life.
— Combination of individual approach and insertion into a group in a socialising and motivating environment.
— Cooperation with various institutions to look at personal, family, social and health problems that may lie behind the 'school' problem.
— Active not passive consumption; and self-assessment-based evaluation of progress made, 'constructive learning'.
— Flexible curriculum and timetable.

—  Educators as mediators.
—  Attention to languages, new information technologies and computers.
—  'Teaching contract'.
—  Some elements of the programme inside businesses.
—  Guidance, character, attitude and self-esteem development.
—  Premises and image of the school less-scholastic, closer to the natural environment of the youngsters yet still free of parental control.

### 2.4.  Scheduling and length of the action

The first beneficiaries of the action began to come to the Second Chance School of Bilbao on 4 November 1997.

The duration was initially set for the end of 1999.

### 2.5.  Is your action/project in any way part of/supported by a national scheme or legislation that aims to combat social exclusion?

The action is within the framework of the Second Chance Schools European network, promoted by the European Community as part of Objective 3: To combat social exclusion through education and training.

## III.  Partnerships and means used

### 3.1.  Name, status and role of the main partner

The management of the Second Chance School of Bilbao is by Lan-Ekintza Bilbao.

Lan Ekintza — Bilbao, is a municipal company with the task of formulating policy in relation to jobs, developing vocational training and promoting the local economy. Concerning:

—  Unemployed people living in the city who want to take positive steps to further their integration in the job market.
—  Companies, including their workers, working in the area.
—  Those people promoting a business project who have the possibility of creating their own work in the city.

The principal concerns of Lan Ekintza-Bilbao are:

—  Job training and programmes of in-work training.
—  Job orientation and job monitoring.
—  Continuous training and job re-cycling.
—  Acting as an intermediary in the job market.
—  Placements in companies.
—  Aid for the self-employed and for those creating new companies.
—  An informational and guidance service for those creating companies.
—  Courses for new company promoters.
—  A workshop for company promoters.
—  A 'nursery' for new companies.
—  A company initiatives competition.
—  Integrated programmes for intervening in underprivileged areas of the city.

### 3.2.  Other partners

European Software Institute based in metropolitan Bilbao.
Bilbao Metropoli-30 association (RDA with 100 members).
Basque government.
Province of Bizkaia.
*Prospektiker* (research).
Private companies.
Employers organisations.
Universities.
Neighbourhood associations caritas and other NGOs.
All to be placed in a working group and providing input.

### 3.3. Monitoring and ongoing evaluation

Follow-up:
Beneficiaries and tutors make continuous follow-ups with weekly meetings.
Weekly follow-up meetings at Lan Ekintza.
Monitoring forms of the Second Chance Schools European network.

### 3.4. External evaluation of the action

The European Commission itself carries out external assessment, local actors such as the town council, business associations and the Department of Education.

## IV. Resources

### 4.1. Human resources used

Management team of Lan Ekintza-Bilbao: Rikardo Barkala, Marcos Muro, Begoña Andrés and Joseba Egia (supervision and control roles).
Consultant for SCS Bilbao: Eneko Astigarraga.
Responsible in Lan Ekintza-Bilbao structure: Ander.
Director of the School: Txomin Martinez Moreno.
15 tutors. In-company tutors.
10 trainers. Vocational trainers.

### 4.2. Organisational and technical means used

The Second Chance School of Bilbao is located in a former State primary school in the Bilbao La Vieja district, which has been adapted to the needs of the project.
It has several workshops for learning trades, although the beneficiaries are able to use other workshops and installations at Lan Ekintza.
The classrooms are equipped with personal computers (one for every two beneficiaries), and special emphasis is placed on the creation of multimedia materials that facilitate individualised learning. Informatics and multimedia play a central role in that project.
The SCS—Information System—project will enable the creation of an Intranet and Internet between the network of EVTA centres and SCS centres.
The learning of languages should be additional focus of the project.

### 4.3. Financial data

## V. Innovative features of the action

It attempts to provide a solution to the problems of school failure and social exclusion among the more disadvantaged population of the urban areas of Metropolitan Bilbao.
Main innovations:
— Participation of social agents.
— An educational contract.
— Trans-nationality: mobility of the youths.
— European network.
— Individualised tutoring.
— Integrated learning plan: personalised learning adapted to the individual, constructive, functional learning, cooperative, interactive learning, and global, interdisciplinary learning.
— Vocational guidance counselling.
— Fostering of self-knowledge and self-esteem.

## VI. Comments

# I. Brief description of the action

## 1.1. Name of the project
EPES. Psycho-educative intervention programme with young people with social, family related and professional difficulties to integration.

## 1.2. Organisation undertaking the action
Council of Abrera (Barcelona), Justice Department (Autonomous Government of Catalonia), Social Institute (Navarra).

## 1.3. Address
Copsa Provenza 122.
City: Barcelona 08029. Country: Spain.
Tel: (34-93) 322 08 88. Fax: (34-93) 322 10 05.
E-mail: copsa@grn.es
Contact: Miriaim Diez Pinol.

## 1.4. Brief description of the action:
The goal of the EPES programme is to give some psycho-educative instructions to the professionals of the education, social services and fathers, to help the integral development of the youth. The results of the educational method EPES are reflected in:
(i) increasing the capacity of the professionals to work with young people and to help the fathers and mothers;
(ii) improvement in the social and education-related factors which are necessary for the development to the youth;
(iii) better insertion of young people in training processes;
(iv) global development of the youth.

# II. Approach and content

## 2.1. Context, motivation and origin of the initiative
The education and social services professionals have difficult working situations/conditions. This affects directly the training, education and development of the youth.

## 2.2. Target group (socially excluded youth, long-term unemployed, etc.; give ages and details of the populations concerned; their status)
Professionals of the education and social services (public and private institutions); disaffected youth; youth workers and social helpers.

## 2.3. Socio-educational approach
The EPES programme introduces a new psycho-educative method. This allows adapting to the educational needs and learning capabilities of each youth in a tailor-made manner.

## 2.4. Scheduling and length of the action
Duration: 10 years.
Development: Local. Towns with important pockets of juvenile delinquency and youth unemployment.

## 2.5. Is your action/project in any way part of/supported by a national scheme or legislation that aims to combat social exclusion?
Programme implemented at national level (Spain).

### III. Partnerships and means used

**3.1. Name, status and role of the main partner**
Direction and planning the project. Training the educators. Evaluation of the programme.

**3.2. Other partners**
Social education institutions in Navarra. Schools in Catalonia.
Radios (national area) in Spain.

**3.3. Monitoring and ongoing evaluation**
Interview the professionals (tutors).
*Pares Diagramme.*
Monitoring of behaviour of pupils (at school, work and at home).

**3.4. External evaluation of the action**
Universities of Catalonia (UAB).

### IV. Resources

**4.1. Human resources used**
Psychologist (10).
Experts in Pedagogy (8).
Teachers (4).

**4.2. Organisational and technical means used**
Classroom.
Practical exercises.
Tutorial and individual treatment and control in the job.

**4.3. Financial data**

### V. Innovative features of the action

The idea of the EPES project is to have a new psycho-educational method to solve the difficulties of the educators in treating the problems of the young people. In the institutions where EPES have been applied, there has been a diminished absence of the teachers. At the same time, there has been a marked positive change in the anti-social behaviour of the young people. The coordination between school and family was better.

### VI. Comments

The application of the EPES programme has been at local level. So, its methodology can be useful in other countries. For this reason, COPSA is actually in contact with European institutions active in this field of training, and qualifying professionals in the field of fighting social exclusion.

# I. Brief description of the action

### 1.1. Name of the project
Integration of apprentices in craft workshops.

### 1.2. Organisation undertaking the action
Seville's municipal council department responsible for economic and tourist matters *(excmo ayto)*.

### 1.3. Address
City: Seville-41013. Country: Spain.
Tel.: (345-95) 459 09 24. Fax:
E-mail: aytosevillaadapt@spaincon.es
Contact: Enrique Parilla.

### 1.4. Brief description of the action
Recruitment of 10 young people aged 16 to 21 as apprentices in 10 craft workshops selected beforehand in the San Luis de la Alameda district. The project is designed to integrate unemployed young people into the world of work and at the same time to safeguard the traditional craft trades and the concept of apprenticeship.


# II. Approach and content

### 2.1. Context, motivation and origin of the initiative
Enhancement of the traditional craft trades which have always existed in the San Luis de la Alameda district, in order to promote the occupational integration of young people and to consolidate these traditional trades.

### 2.2. Target group (socially excluded youth, long-term unemployed, etc.; give ages and details of the populations concerned; their status)
Unemployed young persons aged 16 to 21 with a very low level of training and problems getting into the employment market.

### 2.3. Socio-educational approach
The apprentices will receive theoretical and practical training from a trainer/coordinator in conjunction with the craftsman running the workshop, thus enhancing the young person's chances of getting into a job.

### 2.4. Scheduling and length of the action
Six-month recruitment of 10 young people who will receive theoretical and practical training in a specific trade from a trainer/coordinator. The training will take place in the actual workshops in conjunction with the owners.

### 2.5. Is your action/project in any way part of/supported by a national scheme or legislation that aims to combat social exclusion?
This project must fit into the San Luis de la Alameda urban community programme.


# III. Partnerships and means used

### 3.1. Name, status and role of the main partner
No partners.

### 3.2. Other partners

### 3.3. Monitoring and ongoing evaluation

Continuous evaluation throughout the project, based on three-monthly reports. A questionnaire to be completed by the craftsmen and apprentices alike will form the basis of the final report.

### 3.4. External evaluation of the action

None.

## IV. Resources

### 4.1. Human resources used

One teaching specialist who will act as project leader; one tutor/coordinator for each workshop; nine craftsmen.

### 4.2. Organisational and technical means used

The apprenticeship will take place in existing craft workshops. CAD software will be used in the teaching.

### 4.3. Financial data

Estimate of the cost of the action:

Overall: ESP 10.2 million (ECU 61 818).

When distinguishing various financial contributions and making available of technical and human means:

— in investment terms

— in operating costs:

one instructor: ESP 3 million.

recruitment of 10 apprentices: ESP 4.2 million.

miscellaneous: ESP 300 000.

## V. Innovative features of the action

The innovative feature of the programme is the endeavour to perpetuate craft trades that are in danger of disappearing through lack of private initiative, at the same time safeguarding the concept of apprenticeship.

## VI. Comments

# I. Brief description of the action

### 1.1. Name of the project
*Programa de Innovación Metodológica para la Educación y Reinserción de Adultos (Primera).*

### 1.2. Organisation undertaking the action
*Centro Español de Solidaridad — Proyecto Hombre.*

### 1.3. Address
c/o Martín de los Meros, 68.
City: Madrid. Country: Spain.
Tel: (34-(91) 542-35 07. Fax: (34-(91) 542 46 93.
E-mail: proy.hom@lander.es
Contact: Javier Ibanez.

### 1.4. Brief description of the action
The priority of the project is to combat exclusion by promoting access to training for the underprivileged by means of a curriculum structure to provide a vocational qualification, and an innovative methodology that seeks to pursue and supplement the guidelines established by the therapeutic community.

# II. Approach and content

### 2.1. Context, motivation and origin of the initiative
*Proyecto Hombre*, a therapeutic and educational programme whose ultimate objective is the social rehabilitation of drug addicts, has extended its activities so as to also include training of this target group with a view to reinsertion on the labour market.

### 2.2. Target group (socially excluded youth, long-term unemployed, etc.; give ages and details of the populations concerned; their status)
Drug addicts, of which 50 % have a criminal record.

### 2.3. Socio-educational approach
Some 30 % have been out of work for over three years; 23.8 % started to work illegally before they reached the age of 14. The unemployment rate of the population starting on *Proyecto Hombre* 98, was 38 %. Important school failure: 39 % did not achieve the minimum official qualification.

### 2.4. Scheduling and length of the action
Three years. The project consists of structuring two complementary parts:
— curriculum structure: basic vocational training, vocational qualification, personal occupational and social training and guidance;
— didactical working methodology.

### 2.5. Is your action/project in any way part of/supported by a national scheme or legislation that aims to combat social exclusion?

# III. Partnerships and means used

### 3.1. Name, status and role of the main partner
*Proyecto Hombre Madrid* — coordinator of the project. Developed the methodology and it will be tested in the therapeutic community

**3.2.** **Other partners**
*Centro di Solidarità di Modena* — Training for trainer and together with the *Institut* de *Pedagogie Du Projet*. Reviewing the work with the reinsertion team to discover the underlying pedagogy.

**3.3.** **Monitoring and ongoing evaluation**
University of Bologna; will take care of evaluation.

**3.4.** **External evaluation of the action**

## IV. Resources

**4.1.** **Human resources used**
Two experts in developed educational methodology. Educators and experts. Therapists for reinsertion of drug addicts.

**4.2.** **Organisational and technical means used**

**4.3.** **Financial data**
Estimate of the cost of the action:
* overall
  ESP 178 460
* when distinguishing various financial contributions and making available of technical and human means:
  — in investment terms: ESP 150 150
  — in operating costs:  ESP 27 510.

## V. Innovative features of the action
A methodology to analyse the educational needs on the basis of the systems of rehabilitation used in the therapeutic process in their translation to the curricula applied in the project. A curriculum structure designed for favouring personal independence, the basis for social rehabilitation.

## VI. Comments

# Sweden

## I. Brief description of the action

### 1.1. Name of the project
*'Villa Fridhem'*.

### 1.2. Organisation undertaking the action
The Education Board in Härnösand (Director of Education — Dan Holmberg).

### 1.3. Address
Cityhuset, Storgatan 30, S-871 31.
City: Härnösand. Country: Sweden.
Tel.: (46-611) 280 00. Fax: (46-611) 281 45.
Contact: Gunnar Orving.
E-mail: orving@aurora.borealis.se

### 1.4. Brief description of the action
Restoration by young people of a preservation-classed building in Härnösand. Guidance and training by local and regional craftsmen and experts in the field of preservation. The project and the building will serve as a basis for future actions for 15 to 24 year old people.

## II. Approach and content

### 2.1. Context, motivation and origin of the initiative
Local initiative to cope with the growing rate of unemployed young people. The ambition to forward local tradition and skills of craftsmanship to the young generation.

### 2.2. Target group (socially excluded youth, long-term unemployed, etc.; give ages and details of the populations concerned; their status)
Unemployed young people lacking basic education, 15 to 24 years of age.

### 2.3. Socio-educational approach
Individual learning plans integrated in and linked to secondary and upper secondary school programmes including counselling service.

### 2.4. Scheduling and length of the action
Three years.

### 2.5. Is your action/project in any way part of/supported by a national scheme or legislation that aims to combat social exclusion?
Selected as one out of five projects accepted for funding by the Swedish National Board for Youth Affairs (*Ungdomsstyrelsen*) — Education — Training — Youth.

## III.    Partnerships and means used

**3.1.    Name, status and role of the main partner**
See 2.5 above.

**3.2.    Other partners**
Local partners from different sectors of the community constitute the steering group.

**3.3.    Monitoring and ongoing evaluation**
The steering group and the Education Board in Härnösand.

**3.4.    External evaluation of the action**
The Swedish National Board for Youth Affairs.

## IV.    Resources

**4.1.    Human resources used**
The steering group and the project leader, personnel from the school sector (teachers, counsellors) and the social sector, the local employment office, craftsmen, experts on preservation.

**4.2.    Organisational and technical means used**

**4.3.    Financial data**
Estimate of the cost of the action:
- overall, ECU 200 000 + local costs for 'human resources';

## V.    Innovative features of the action

Local initiative based on learning and integration for 'normality'. Young people forming their own new individual platforms and a basis for future actions and entrepreneurship linked to culture, internationalisation, exchange activities and tourism in the community.

## VI.    Comments

# The Netherlands

## I. Brief description of the action

**1.1. Name of the project**
Spin Web.

**1.2. Organisation undertaking the action**
PDI Amsterdam West.

**1.3. Address**
Louis Couperustraatt 131.
City: 1064BE Amsterdam. Country: The Netherlands.
Tel: (31-20) 614-5047. Fax: (31-20) 614-5633.
E-mail: europpi@xsl.all.nl
Contact: Ed Dykstra.

**1.4. Brief description of the action**
Building up and creating a school career centre in a cooperative relationship between: a youth help organisation (FPI), a vocational school (NOVA), and the Moroccan Council of Amsterdam for youngsters at risk, with an ethnic minority background.

## II. Approach and content

**2.1. Context, motivation and origin of the initiative**
The target group leaves school without (start) qualifications and doesn't know how to manage in society because of demotivation, negative results and achievements with wrong choice of the vocational direction as the basic element.

**2.2. Target group (socially excluded youth, long-term unemployed, etc.; give ages and details of the populations concerned; their status)**
Youngsters at risk of becoming school dropouts.

**2.3. Socio-educational approach**
Screening and diagnoses.
Social and application training skills.
Orientation on vocation; multimedia training.

**2.4. Scheduling and length of the action**
Screening and orientation (about eight weeks).
Education and vocational training to the end of 1999.
Length of the project: 1998 to 31 December 1999.

**2.5.** **Is your action/project in any way part of/supported by a national scheme or legislation that aims to combat social exclusion?**

## III. Partnerships and means used

**3.1.** **Name, status and role of the main partner**
Esprit-Nova Equal partner Education School (local level).
East Birmingham College trans-national partner. New technology.

**3.2.** **Other partners**
*SMR Stedelyte Marokkaanse Raad*, participation of Moroccan partners.
*Jugend Berufsschulle* — Thüringen.

**3.3.** **Monitoring and ongoing evaluation**
Secretary group will monitor in TMTs.

**3.4.** **External evaluation of the action**

## IV. Resources

**4.1.** **Human resources used**
Youth workers, psychologists, pedagogues and teachers, plus a Moroccan welfare worker.

**4.2.** **Organisational and technical means used**
New centre will be organised in NOVA with multimedia facilities in general as well as new technology vocational skills in a more specific way.

**4.3.** **Financial data**
Combination of own means of PPI as well as of Esprit-NOVA with ESF YouthStart money.

## V. Innovative features of the action
Cooperation of three different organisations with the same target group.
Implementation of new technology into a vocational educational school system.

## VI. Comments

# I. Brief description of the action

### 1.1. Name of the project
Development of courses on assistants level.

### 1.2. Organisation undertaking the action
ROC (Regional Education Centre) Utrecht.

### 1.3. Address
PO Box 3065.
City: 3502 GB Utrecht. Country: The Netherlands.
Tel.: (31 30) 287-7700. Fax: (31-30) 288-3899.
E-mail: norbert.ruepert@wxs.nl
Contact: Norbert Ruepert.

### 1.4. Brief description of the action
Development of courses on the level of assistant in vocational courses. These courses with the maximum duration of one year are targeting young people with learning/social/ behavioural problems. By bringing different disciplines together a new approach to vocational courses is tested.

# II. Approach and content

### 2.1. Context, motivation and origin of the initiative
A large group of especially young people and adults from general adult education who were not able to continue into vocational education as the levels were too high and the courses were not catering to their specific needs. A project was started to develop these courses in three vocational areas following a national qualification (level 1). By bringing expertise from adult education, general education for difficult young people and vocational education together a new approach to these courses was developed.

### 2.2. Target group (socially excluded youth, long-term unemployed, etc.; give ages and details of the populations concerned; their status)
Young people with learning/social/ behavioural problems aged 16 to 22, many from ethnic minorities.
Adults with little or no formal education, also many from ethnic minorities.
Dropouts from other vocational courses.

### 2.3. Socio-educational approach
The main principle is practice before theory; theory is taught through practical work.
Courses are individual, geared to specific needs.
Dutch as a foreign language and vocational language are combined.

### 2.4. Scheduling and length of the action
Courses have started from February 1998. The project will last until the end of this year.

### 2.5. Is your action/project in any way part of/supported by a national scheme or legislation that aims to combat social exclusion?
The qualifications for these courses have been developed nationally and are available for many different vocational areas.

# III. Partnerships and means used

### 3.1. Name, status and role of the main partner
ROC Utrecht, with more than 2 500 students is one of the largest colleges for vocational and adult education in the Netherlands.

### 3.2. Other partners
Businesses in the area, the employment agency and social services in Utrecht.

### 3.3. Monitoring and ongoing evaluation
Regular evaluations and monitoring of students.

### 3.4. External evaluation of the action
At the end a general evaluation will be made as a report to the Ministry of Education.

# IV. Resources

### 4.1. Human resources used
About 15 teachers and five support staff are involved. They have all been trained to work with these groups and are assisted by the pedagogical department of the college of higher education.

### 4.2. Organisational and technical means used
This project has developed social teaching materials, and special classrooms/workshops are used.

### 4.3. Financial data
Investment of the college and of the Ministry is about ECU 250 000. Operating costs are the same as other vocational courses but the college receives extra funding for every individual student.

# V. Innovative features of the action
Bringing together different disciplines in vocational and non-vocational areas. New methods of teaching. Different methods of assessment.

# VI. Comments

# I. Brief description of the action

### 1.1. Name of the project
Assessment used for young people who lack basic skills and qualifications.

### 1.2. Organisation undertaking the action
*OnderwijsGroep Haaglanden.*

### 1.3. Address
Sammersweg 2.2285 SB Rijswijk.
City: Rijswijk. Country: The Netherlands.
Tel: (31-70) 329 89 01. Fax: (31-70) 321 03 08.
E-mail: roctvt@bart.nl
Contact: Jan Van Putten.

### 1.4. Brief description of the action
Assessment used for young people (15 to 25) who lack basic skills and qualifications, is a programme of one week. It is an instrument which enables you to assess (judge/value) the possibilities and limitations of an individual regarding employability and education. The assessment programme contains tests (mostly simulation exercises) on different fields: level of Dutch, arithmetic, technical, physical, social and learning skills, behaviour, professional attitude, personal qualities. It results in advice for further education and profession.

# II. Approach and content

### 2.1. Context, motivation and origin of the initiative
The assessment programme is developed following a request of the employment service bureau (Department of Labour). They had a lot of young people in their card cabinet (most of them dropouts) and didn't know what to do with them: send them to school for a vocational training course, let them do mental or physical labour, etc.
Now we use this programme within our school for vocational education as an instrument of selection: to give younger people who lack basic skills and qualifications new chances, to prevent dropout and to solve the dropout problem. The profit for the school is an increasing output.

### 2.2. Target group (socially excluded youth, long-term unemployed, etc.; give ages and details of the populations concerned; their status)
At our school for vocational education we use the assessment as a programme for people who:
— Are socially excluded because they dropped out of secondary school, have a lack of basic skills, a lot of social and emotional problems, sometimes have a record of criminal activity, but they still want a qualification and aren't accepted by any vocational training.
— Don't get in their chosen vocational training because they aren't qualified.
— Can't make their choice of a profession and vocational education.
— Made a wrong choice or don't fit in their vocational training they are following.
  Aged between 15 and 25 years.

### 2.3. Socio-educational approach
We explain in the introduction that taking part in the assessment programme is their own choice and responsibility. They are told that everything they do or don't do is telling something about themselves and can have its consequences for the report and our advice for further education or profession. We are neither educators nor teachers: we just attend the assessment programme and observe them.
Most of our candidates accept full responsibility and do the best they can.

**2.4.** **Scheduling and length of the action**

The assessment programme takes one week with 15 candidates in one group. The average is one group every week during the year. From June till January 1997 we served 365 candidates.

**2.5.** **Is your action/project in any way part of/supported by a national scheme or legislation that aims to combat social exclusion?**

No.

## III. Partnerships and means used

**3.1.** **Name, status and role of the main partner**

Until now, no partners. We will try to interest a Norwegian college. Contact has been made.

**3.2.** **Other partners**

**3.3.** **Monitoring and ongoing evaluation**

Monitoring by project leader.

**3.4.** **External evaluation of the action**

## IV. Resources

**4.1.** **Human resources used**

The assessment team consists of one project leader and six professionally trained attendants covering the different fields the assessment programme contains. They work part time for the assessment programme and work also as teachers within different vocational courses. The team contains a test-psychologist who is also a teacher of Dutch and arithmetic. Two teachers to teach social behaviour/social skills, who also work, respectively, as an actress and as a director in a commercial context. One of them has a lot of experience in youth assistance/guidance.

A sports teacher, who is also a soccer trainer, ski instructor, etc.

Two drawing teachers, for manipulative and technical skills who are sculptors in their spare time. The project leader is a Dutch teacher, she studied pedagogy and has worked for several years in the youth assistance/guidance, and is a supervisor for teachers in secondary education.

**4.2.** **Organisational and technical means used**

We are trying to get IT tests (or develop them ourselves).

**4.3.** **Financial data**

At the moment the overall costs per year are about NLG 250 000 (mostly personnel costs).

## V. Innovative features of the action

The programme we have developed is a basic programme of one week. We aim to give younger people who had lost all trace, in a very short time, a new workable perspective in a profession or education.

We want to make specific assessment programmes applicable for specific directions of vocational education. We made a programme for mechanics before they entered the study. The main purpose is to prevent dropouts and advance the output of this course.

In a very large institution of vocational training we can also develop assessment exercises for our colleges in a development centre in order to put the right person in the right place.

## VI. Comments

No comments.

# I. Brief description of the action

### 1.1. Name of the project
'Bridging the Gap'.

### 1.2. Organisation undertaking the action
DSO — (Municipal Educational Service of the city of Rotterdam).

### 1.3. Address
Postbox 70014 3000 KS Rotterdam.
City: Rotterdam. Country: The Netherlands.
Tel.: (31-10) 417 34 96. Fax: (31-10) 414 3162.
E-mail: rfd@euronet.nl
Contact: Robert Dekker.

### 1.4. Brief description of the action
A broad action in secondary and vocational schools in the city of Rotterdam (NL) with the goals: monitoring of students, preventing school failure, improving the quality of schools, analysing patterns of school failure, preventing absenteeism, facilitating the transfer to the labour market.

# II. Approach and content

### 2.1. Context, motivation and origin of the initiative
In the city of Rotterdam (110 000 students) the average level of education is low, the number of dropouts is too high, the number of unemployed persons is too high. This was the motivation for action.

### 2.2. Target group (socially excluded youth, long-term unemployed, etc.; give ages and details of the populations concerned; their status)
Target group: at-risk students, students from minority groups, socially excluded youth. Ages 14 to 21 years. About 60 % out of minority groups.

### 2.3. Socio-educational approach
Actions in schools, preventing absenteeism, social care, specific training of students, teachers and social welfare workers.

### 2.4. Scheduling and length of the action
1998-2002.

### 2.5. Is your action/project in any way part of/supported by a national scheme or legislation that aims to combat social exclusion?
There are special measures for combating inner city problems.

# III. Partnerships and means used

### 3.1. Name, status and role of the main partner
DRD — Department of education of the city of Rotterdam in cooperation with private school boards.

### 3.2. Other partners
School boards health service, social welfare, and school advisory service.

### 3.3. Monitoring and ongoing evaluation
There is an extensive system of monitoring and evaluation. Publications are realised on local and national level.

### 3.4. External evaluation of the action

Three university institutions are under contract.

## IV. Resources

### 4.1. Human resources used

More than 40 people are involved.

### 4.2. Organisational and technical means used

Modern office facilities (local government facilities).

### 4.3. Financial data

Estimate of the cost of the action:
- Overall: ECU 3 million.
- When distinguishing various financial contributions and making available of technical and human means:
  — in investment terms: 40 %
  — in operating costs: 60 %.

## V. Innovative features of the action

1. High quality level of monitoring and quality improvement.
2. Quick action and immediate response.
3. State of art of using ICT.
4. Innovative analysis of patterns of failure, strategic analysis and strategic planning.

## VI. Comments

We have a profound desire to share knowledge, experience with other European partners.

# United Kingdom

## I.  Brief description of the action

### 1.1.  Name of the project

### 1.2.  Organisation undertaking the action
City of Sunderland Council supported by two external consultants.

### 1.3.  Address
Civic centre, PO Box 100. Sunderland, UK.
Tel.: (44-191) 553 11 56. Fax: (44-191) 553 11 59.
E-mail: maria.rofa@sunderland.gov.uk
Contact: John Thurlbeck.

### 1.4.  Brief description of the action
To review all services provided by City Council to young people, identifying:
— the quality of existing provisions;
— the gaps in existing provision for young people;
— the solutions to the gaps identified.
Phase I: service providers; Phase II: young people; Phase III: recommendation.

## II.  Approach and content

### 2.1.  Context, motivation and origin of the initiative
Council members' desire to provide better services to young people and to ensure their social inclusion through a 'corporate youth strategy'.

### 2.2.  Target group (socially excluded youth, long-term unemployed, etc.; give ages and details of the populations concerned; their status)
Young people aged 11 and 21, particularly disaffected/alienated/disengaged young people 16 to 19 years old.

### 2.3.  Socio-educational approach
Corporate policy overview, supported by a dynamic and responsive Youth Service, which addresses young people through 'informal education' routes plus youth work approaches in schools, colleges, housing, social services.

### 2.4.  Scheduling and length of the action
Review took six months, 6/97–12/97; implementation beginning May 1998: youth service five years development plans/responses 98/02; plus individual departmental action plans/responses by Youth Strategy Policy Officer.

**2.5.** **Is your action/project in any way part of/supported by a national scheme or legislation, which aims to combat social exclusion? Please describe:**

It fits with the 'Prime Minister's Social Exclusion Unit', Green Paper on lifelong learning, European ESF Objective 2 and, some Community Initiatives for young people (Leonardo da Vinci, Socrates, Employment) and Second Chance School; White Paper on teaching and learning; Single Regeneration Budget, Welfare to Work (New Deal), National Plan for European 1998 Employment Policy, Government New Start Strategy, Sunderland Telematic Strategy and other European and national government policies regarding social regeneration, education, and young people.

## III.   Partnerships and means used

**3.1.** **Name, status and role of the main partner:**

City of Sunderland Council.

**3.2.** **Other partners:**

City of Sunderland College (six centres across the city); University of Sunderland; Northumbria Police; Sunderland Health Authority; City Hospital Trust; Priority Health Care Wearside; Voluntary Youth Sector Forum; Sunderland City Training and Enterprise Council.

**3.3.** **Monitoring and ongoing evaluation (monitoring, reporting tools):**

Three phased reports, monthly working group meetings, quarterly steering group meetings, Young Peoples Forums and police officer reports.

**3.4.** **External evaluation of the action:**

Carried by two external consultants, report reviewed by National Youth Agency (report) and further National Conference on Best Practice, which was held in Sunderland in the summer of 1998.

## IV.   Resources

**4.1.** **Human resources used:**

Variety of City Council staff, police, probation service, college lecturers, Health Authority workers, freelance consultants, teachers, young people and youth workers.

**4.2.** **Organisational and technical means used:**

Paper base, information technology, meetings, focus groups, seminars, workshops, conference, 8 November 1997, questionnaires/surveys, interviews.

**4.3.** **Financial data:**

The Youth Review (six months) overall: GBP 120 000. Planned commitment from the Chief Executive's Department in 1998/99: GBP 250 000. Looking for extra money from other departments. Project implementation will have individual budgets applied to them and will look for individual external funds.

Minimum overall budget estimated to meet minimum demands, likely to be approximately GBP 3 million (new money/new activities around GBP 1.5 millions).

## V.   Innovative features of the action

It involves young people throughout with a bottom approach.

It seeks to address real, not perceived need.

It involves critical analysis of all services at one time.

It seeks to develop a dynamic strategy policy for dealing with the social exclusion of young people.

It seeks to re-engage young people in local democracy and open and transparent governance.

## VI.     Comments

There is a close link between the outcomes of the youth reviews and current pilot projects such as 'Solutions Project' (second chance model); 'Young Adult Learners Project'; 'Youth Asian Voices'. We would be able to do a 10 minute presentation on number 6 (The territorial dimension – local partnership).

## I. Brief description of the action

### 1.1. Name of the project
Socrates Basic Skills Project.

### 1.2. Organisation undertaking the action
Lewisham College, UK.

### 1.3. Address
Lewisham Way.
City: London SE4 1UT. Country: UK.
Tel.: (44-181) 694 32 71. Fax: (44-181) 694 91 63.
E-mail: dho@staff.lewisham.ac.uk
Contact: David Horsburgh.

### 1.4. Brief description of the action
The Socrates project is a review of multimedia-based materials aimed at developing literacy skills, and is being undertaken in all the participating countries. It is intended that guidelines should be developed for the production of learning materials to accompany selected CD-ROM-based multimedia resources. We are also interested in finding the best ways in which teachers can use such resources to achieve successful learning experiences for their students.

## II. Approach and content

### 2.1. Context, motivation and origin of the initiative
It arose from some work done at Lewisham College within a resource-based learning project. This explored the use of the New Reading Disk which was produced by Cambridge Training and Development and the Basic Skills Agency. Young learners wishing to develop basic literacy skills used the resource. During the project it was discovered that the CD-ROM needed to be accompanied with high-quality learning materials that could help structure the activities of the student.

### 2.2. Target group (socially excluded youth, long-term unemployed, etc.; give ages and details of the populations concerned; their status)
The students we are particularly interested in using these resources often have problems with basic reading, writing and communication. These problems will often be a barrier to employment and can serve to exclude individuals from many normal day-to-day activities. In Lewisham College we are particularly interested in working with the 16- to 19-year-old group who have special educational needs. Among our partners there is interest in adult literacy development.

### 2.3. Socio-educational approach
Many of our students would be from socially excluded groups on the basis of ethnic origin, special learning needs, socio-economic grouping and general educational disadvantage. Learning processes would be designed to be non-discriminatory and inclusive.

### 2.4. Scheduling and length of the action
Year 1. Identification of user needs. Review of current relevant multimedia. Development of multimedia evaluation methodologies. Development of teaching Materials. Choice of suitable multimedia to develop literacy skills.
Year 2. Piloting chosen multimedia resources with learners, examining pedagogic process in detail in a number of test sites. Improving teaching materials, dissemination of findings via Internet and events.

**2.5.** **Is your action/project in any way part of/supported by a national scheme or legislation that aims to combat social exclusion?**

It is currently a national priority by the UK government to combat social exclusion. Our project contributes to local work in our college on the 'New Deal'.

## III. Partnerships and means used

**3.1.** **Name, status and role of the main partner**

Lewisham College.
Further Education College in the UK.

**3.2.** **Other partners**

*INETI Instituto Nacional de Endenharia e Tecnologia Industrial* — Portugal.
Karkku College of Home Economics and Social Services — Finland.
*Volkshochschule Florisdorf* — Austria.

**3.3.** **Monitoring and ongoing evaluation**

Three transnational meetings to review progress. Project manager visits each partner to monitor and report.

**3.4.** **External evaluation of the action**

We have asked the National Multimedia Consortium in the UK to evaluate our first year report and ongoing work.

## IV. Resources

**4.1.** **Human resources used**

A project manager, a number of teachers. Dedicated researchers in UK and Portugal. Learning facilitators in the UK.

**4.2.** **Organisational and technical means used**

Usage of multimedia computers and CD-ROM-based software in classrooms and learning centres.

**4.3.** **Financial data**

Estimate of the cost of the action:
Overall for 1997/98: ECU 206 000 (of which ECU 100 000 is grant allocation).
Estimated for 1998/99: ECU 225 758.
1998 grant requested ECU 134 239.
Most money spent on operating costs. Some investment in new hardware (one computer) and the software that we have been evaluating.

## V. Innovative features of the action

The project mainly concentrates on learning and not only the technology that mediates this learning
The project is introducing a number of teachers to action research.
There is a consideration of both learners and teachers needs.
Good practice should be developed for the evaluation of basic skills, literacy, multimedia and the development of learning materials for this area.

## VI. Comments

We aim to link with a Leonardo project developing the use of the New Reading Disk and on line technology to provide training for in basic skills for SMEs. This is based at Lancaster University in the UK.

## I. Brief description of the action

**1.1. Name of the project**
'Year 11 Project'.

**1.2. Organisation undertaking the action**
London Borough of Brent Education Authority.

**5.3. Address**
Chesterfield House, 9 Park Lane.
City: London HA9 7TW. Country: UK.
Tel: (44-181) 205 11 37. Fax: (44-181) 201 31 72.
Contact: Paul Roper.

**1.4. Brief description of the action**
Project designed to provide education and vocational opportunities for young people in their last year of schooling who are not attending a mainstream school, through exclusion.

## II. Approach and content

**2.1. Context, motivation and origin of the initiative**
To provide educational and training opportunities to pupils who would otherwise complete school without any qualifications or choices.

**2.2. Target group (socially excluded youth, long-term unemployed, etc.; give ages and details of the populations concerned; their status)**
Boys and girls aged 14 to 16 (maximum number 50) who are permanently excluded from school.

**2.3. Socio-educational approach**
Combination of academic, personal and social and vocational education.

**2.4. Scheduling and length of the action**
Project of one-year duration for each group.

**2.5. Is your action/project in any way part of/supported by a national scheme or legislation that aims to combat social exclusion?**
Project falls within government policies to combat social exclusion and local education authority behaviour management plan.

## III. Partnerships and means used

**3.1. Name, status and role of the main partner**
Brent Pupil Referral Unit.

**3.2. Other partners**
College of North West London, Brent & Harrow Work Experience Consortium, Lifetime Careers, Northwest London Tec.

**3.3. Monitoring and ongoing evaluation**
Three times annually by advisory board meetings, reporting to the Director of Education and the local council.

**3.4. External evaluation of the action**
Office for standards in education (Ofsted) regular inspections.

## IV.      Resources

**4.1.    Human resources used**
Teachers (7), welfare officer (1), administration (1).

**4.2.    Organisational and technical means used**
Dedicated building, plus access to college and other local facilities.

**4.3.    Financial data**
Estimate of the cost of the action:
- overall GBP 400 000.

## V.      Innovative features of the action

The project aims to provide a systematic approach to reducing exclusions from mainstream school and to ensure that pupils excluded from school have more opportunities and choices for increasing their life chances.

## VI.      Comments

We would welcome the opportunity for participating in networking and information exchanges, and for further developing the scope of our work.

## I. Brief description of the action

**1.1. Name of the project**
Pilton Project: Early Intervention (Evaluation).

**1.2. Organisation undertaking the action**
External evaluation — (Helen Fraser) Moray House Institute of Education.
Project development: Local education authority (Edinburgh).

**1.3. Address**
Moray House Institute of Education, Holyrood Road.
City: Edinburgh. Country: Scotland, UK.
Tel.: (44-131) 55869 97. Fax: (44-131) 557 49 62.
E-mail: helen.fraser@mhie.ac.uk
Contact: Helen Fraser.

**1.4. Brief description of the action**
Major early intervention in literacy in an area of multiple disadvantages in Edinburgh.
A two-year project with both quantitative and qualitative data gathered in internal and external evaluation.

## II. Approach and content

**2.1. Context, motivation and origin of the initiative**
Local authority area initiative — schools and community.

**2.2. Target group (socially excluded youth, long-term unemployed, etc.; give ages and details of the populations concerned; their status)**
Children aged five to eight and also an adult education initiative toward literacy.

**2.3. Socio-educational approach**
Integrative across different agencies: education and community.

**2.4. Scheduling and length of the action**
From 1993-1995 then a further development to 1997. Since then the Scottish Office (Government) has financed a national initiative (GBP 24 000 000) and I have the evaluation contract for that.

**2.5. Is your action/project in any way part of/supported by a national scheme or legislation that aims to combat social exclusion?**
Yes, there is a three-year Scottish programme on literacy and numeracy intervention (1998-2002). Helen Fraser has the joint directorship of the evaluation.

## III. Partnerships and means used

**3.1. Name, status and role of the main partner**

**3.2. Other partners**

**3.3. Monitoring and ongoing evaluation**

**3.4. External evaluation of the action**
As above.

## IV. Resources

### 4.1. Human resources used
Pilton: various.

### 4.2. Organisational and technical means used

### 4.3. Financial data
Estimate of the cost of the action: GBP 250 000   (Pilton: Edinburgh).

## V. Innovative features of the action
This project was a leader for the current government national initiative in Scotland.

## VI. Comments
The Early Intervention work now operating across Scotland has a high political profile and our evaluation of the earlier Pilton project has developed our involvement to a national level.

## I. Brief description of the action

### 1.1. Name of the project
Rewarding and Widening Achievement: Personal, Social and Key Skills Accreditation.

### 1.2. Organisation undertaking the action
Award Scheme Development and Accreditation Network (ASDAN).

### 1.3. Address
C/o 27 Redland Hill, Redland.
City: Bristol. Country: UK.
Tel.: (44-117) 923 98 43. Fax: (44-117) 946 77 74.
Contact: Dave Brockington.

### 1.4. Brief description of the action:
A national programme based at the University of the West of England (providing for over 100 000 learners each year, mainly in the 14 to 25 age range) combining activity-based curriculum with a framework for developing and assessing key skills with an emphasis on negotiation, cooperation and rewarding achievement.

## II. Approach and content

### 2.1. Context, motivation and origin of the initiative
Designed as an experiential learning programme for the development and assessment of personal, social, key and employability skills. It is intended to accredit and give recognition to those areas not formally addressed and certified outside of the subjects of the UK National Curriculum.

### 2.2. Target group (socially excluded youth, long-term unemployed, etc.; give ages and details of the populations concerned; their status)
All ability range, especially useful as a motivational vehicle for under-achieving school age (secondary) pupils and disaffected 14 to 16 year olds. Also heavy usage in the 16 to 19-year-olds in the UK further education sector. Also used alongside vocational programmes prior and post for 16 year olds. Work also with homeless young people aged 18 to 25 and mentally ill.

### 2.3. Socio-educational approach
Experiential learning/small steps of achievement/formative assessment/confidence building.

### 2.4. Scheduling and length of the action
Year-long programmes with progression for ages 14 to 18+ intended to contribute to the achievement of the UK National Training and Education Targets.

### 2.5. Is your action/project in any way part of/supported by a national scheme or legislation that aims to combat social exclusion?
We are a national scheme aiming to develop personal, social and citizenship education. We have no formal Government funding for our central services although our programmes are approved by the Education Ministry for use in schools and colleges.

## III. Partnerships and means used

### 3.1. Name, status and role of the main partner
ASDAN — Educational charity.

**3.2.** **Other partners**
University of the West of England.
Youth Education Service (YES).  Voluntary sector educational charity.

**3.3.** **Monitoring and ongoing evaluation**
Incorporates and implements a national system of moderation and assessment through the key skills standards set by the UK Qualifications and Curriculum Authority (QCA).

**3.4.** **External evaluation of the action**
Independent evaluation conducted (1997) by the Institute of Education of the University of London.

# IV. Resources

**4.1.** **Human resources used**
Central team: 12 persons.
Regional coordinators: approximately 60 persons.
Area coordinators: 8.

**4.2.** **Organisational and technical means used**
Computer network system.
Video conferencing is developed.

**4.3.** **Financial data**
The charity re-invests its income each year into the work.
Turnover GBP 600 000 to 750 000.

# V. Innovative features of the action
1. Accrediting, encouraging and recognising personal and social development.
2. Shifting the focus of empowerment and responsibility for learning to the learner.
3. Formative assessment and modularised; small steps for achievement and progression.
4. Assignment and project-based to encourage active learning.

# VI. Comments

# I.  Brief description of the action

**1.1.  Name of the project**
Schools and community regeneration.

**1.2.  Organisation undertaking the action**
CEDC — Community Education Development Centre.

**1.3.  Address**
Woodway Park School, Wigston Road.
City: Coventry. Country: United Kingdom.
Tel.: (44-1203) 65 57 00. Fax: (44-1203) 65 57 01.
E-mail: paula@cedc.demon.co.uk
Contact: Phil Street.

**1.4.  Brief description of the action**
The project places schools at the centre of a community regeneration strategy.  It is intended schools will be a catalyst for local regeneration.  They will provide local and accessible venues for activities aimed at tackling social exclusion and extending learning opportunities to disaffected groups.


# II.  Approach and content

**2.1.  Context, motivation and origin of the initiative**
The recognition that schools are often the only public resource in disadvantaged communities and they possess under-utilised resources.

**2.2.  Target group (socially excluded youth, long-term unemployed, etc.; give ages and details of the populations concerned; their status)**
Socially excluded young people and long-term unemployed.

**2.3.  Socio-educational approach**
Community approach by schools to encourage participation in learning by socially excluded groups and individuals.

**2.4.  Scheduling and length of the action**
Schools and community regeneration is a three-year project that involves nine UK schools. Each school is establishing a regeneration initiative.

**2.5.  Is your action/project in any way part of/supported by a national scheme or legislation that aims to combat social exclusion?**
This is not supported by a national scheme.


# III.  Partnerships and means used

**3.1.  Name, status and role of the main partner**

**3.2.  Other partners**

**3.3.  Monitoring and ongoing evaluation**
Each school is required to report twice each year.

**3.4.  External evaluation of the action**
Independent evaluation is being carried out by the UK's community development foundation.

## IV. Resources

### 4.1. Human resources used

Human resources include: teachers, adult education tutors, community education workers, youth and community workers.

### 4.2. Organisational and technical means used

New technology, classroom facilities, Outreach bases.

### 4.3. Financial data

Estimate of the cost of the action:

- Overall: GBP 224 000.

## V. Innovative features of the action

The project assists schools to identify their role in the wider regeneration of their community. The project encourages schools to formulate regeneration strategies based on local needs and in partnership with regeneration agencies.

## VI. Comments

This has been a highly successful project that is demonstrating the particular role schools can play in regeneration of their communities.

# I.   Brief description of the action

### 1.1.   Name of the project
1.   Education Initiative.
2.   Wise Start.

### 1.2.   Organisation undertaking the action
Right Track.

### 1.3.   Address
Brook Street Studios, 60 Brook Street, Glasgow, G40 AB, Scotland.
Tel.: (44-141) 556 19 91. Fax: (44-141) 556 19 92.
E-mail: 113335.3140@comp.userve.com
Contact: Caroline Farqhar.

### 1.4.   Brief description of the action
1.   Education Initiative — provides guidance, counselling, inter active learning and action planning for school-aged pupils who refuse to attend school. Includes VQ activity, work experience, mentoring, and family involvement.
2.   Wise Start — similar to above but customised for older age group (16 to 18).


# II.   Approach and content

### 2.1.   Context, motivation and origin of the initiative
Right Track is a charity registered in 1983. Our mission is to provide support to individuals who find it difficult to secure work due to various educational and social disadvantages. We are led by a predominantly private sector Board of Directors.

### 2.2.   Target group (socially excluded youth, long-term unemployed, etc.; give ages and details of the populations concerned; their status)
Education Initiative — 14-, 15- and 16-year-old school refusers. Largely from workless households. Would be classed by school as unable to sit exams. Normally display disruptive behaviour.
Wise Start — 16- to 18-year-olds, 450 clients per annum, 98 % have poor literacy and numeracy skills, 70 % do not reside at home, 78 % are involved in 'recreational drugs', 100 % have no qualifications.

### 2.3.   Socio-educational approach
Social and vocational skills training are integrated. Significant time is spent on individual action planning and the young person taking ownership of their problem. One-to-one work, plus group work. Maximum group size of eight.

### 2.4.   Scheduling and length of the action
Education Initiative —no minimum period. Maximum equals one school year, i.e. three terms.
Wise Start — no minimum period. Maximum equals up to two years.

### 2.5.   Is your action/project in any way part of/supported by a national scheme or legislation that aims to combat social exclusion?  Please describe
Education Initiative  — not part of national scheme.
Wise Start — partly funded by central government Skill-Seekers Initiative, but Right Track secure top-up money for creative elements from private trusts, etc.

## III. Partnerships and means used

### 3.1. Name, status and role of the main partner

Right Track has many partners in delivery of services, i.e. private sector, voluntary sector, health boards, education department, social work, etc. Main funding partners are local economic companies.

### 3.2. Other partners

See above.

### 3.3. Monitoring and ongoing evaluation (monitoring reporting tools)

Variety of tools — reports to committees; external validation; quality control criteria. In Scotland we have a recognised quality management system for education and training called SQMS (Scottish Quality Management System). We comply with all of its standards.

### 3.4. External evaluation of the action

SQMS auditors; Scottish Office; independent consultants.

## IV. Resources

### 4.1. Human resources used (teachers, guardians, etc.)

Ratio of staff to pupils. Education Initiative 1:4: qualified trainers, counsellors and youth workers.
Ratio of young persons Wise Start, 1:8: qualified trainers, counsellors and youth workers.

### 4.2. Organisational and technical means used (facilities, new technology, etc.)

Premises: customised training centre based within local communities. Centres have 'simulated' training.
Rooms for VQ work. Relaxed areas for personal development and computer suites.

### 4.3. Financial data

Cost per pupil on Education Initiative = GBP 187 per week. Capital costs per annum GBP 30 000 for 20 pupils.
Cost per young person per week: Wise Start, GBP 134; Capital cost per 20 young people GBP 50 000.

## V. Innovative features of the action

Education Initiative:
Pupil-led activity and empowerment aspects. Counselling and absence follow-up procedures. Home contact and family centre approach. Core skills training based on survey results from over 200 local employers.
Wise Start integration of non-vocational and vocational training. Customised resources to suit individual needs. 'Simulation training' core skills as above.

## VI. Comments

Right Track helps an average of 500 young people per annum. Over 70 % learn from their experience and move onto work or further training. Drugs, personal hygiene, poor communication skills and homelessness are big issues for Right Track.

# I. Brief description of the action

### 1.1. Name of the project
Rhondda Cynon Taffy Youth Access.

### 1.2. Organisation undertaking the action
Multi-agency partnership.
Lead agencies: local education authority and the Training Enterprise Council.

### 1.3. Address
The Education Centre, Grawen Street, Porth.
City: Mid Glamorgan. Country: South Wales, UK.
Tel: (44-1443) 68 02 12. Fax: (44-1443) 68 02 86.
Contact: Christy Berry.

### 1.4. Brief description of the action
Some 1 120 young people contacted through six different projects. Eighty to attend structured courses (literacy, numeracy, key skills, sport activities); 170 undertake a 'ready for work' scheme; 425 undertake and complete a 'compact' scheme; 445 contacted through Outreach project.

# II. Approach and content

### 2.1. Context, motivation and origin of the initiative
Multi-agencies approach, partly through Children's Services Plan, central government, Community Education Service Plan, Training Enterprise Council.

### 2.2. Target group (socially excluded youth, long-term unemployed, etc.; give ages and details of the populations concerned; their status)
Total population of 15- to 19-year-olds is 14 475. Target 1 100 (7.5 %) who have multiple stresses, low attainment, substance misusers, homeless, poor family relationships, truants, unemployed.

### 2.3. Socio-educational approach
Client centred holistic approach, addressing the multiple needs.

### 2.4. Scheduling and length of the action
Coordinated approach — some projects already ongoing are funded initially until March 1999.

### 2.5. Is your action/project in any way part of/supported by a national scheme or legislation that aims to combat social exclusion?
Youth Access Initiative is a Welsh Office Scheme.

# III. Partnerships and means used

### 3.1. Name, status and role of the main partner
Rhondda Cynon Taff local education authority and Mid-Glamorgan Training Enterprise Council — funding, coordination and service delivery.

### 3.2. Other partners
Colleges, university, employment services, careers, social services, probation, voluntary organisations, Health Authority.

**3.3.    Monitoring and ongoing evaluation**
Quality assessment using OHMCI framework, progress towards agreed targets undertaken via contract reviews.  Customer satisfaction survey.

**3.4.    External evaluation of the action**
Welsh Office.

## IV.    Resources

**4.1.    Human resources used**
Youth workers, business managers, careers officers, teachers, parents, education managers, librarians.

**4.2.    Organisational and technical means used**
Youth centres and schools, use of ICT.

**4.3.    Financial data**
Estimate of the cost of the action: GBP 600 041 (operating costs).

## V.    Innovative features of the action

Business managers mentoring disaffected secondary pupils. Strong multi-agency approaches which links into other youth work provision (GBP 1.3 million).
Training of staff in one or more of the aspects of working with disaffected young people.

## VI.    Comments

The extra external funding has enabled development of this initiative on a strong multi-agency partnership.  It needs to have secure funding for the future if it builds on the good youth work practice already in place.

# I. Brief description of the action

### 1.1. Name of Project
'Encouraging Innovation'.

### 1.2. Organisation
The Institute of Social and Economic Research (INSER).

### 1.3. Address
44 Woodlands Street, Glasgow G62 8NS, Scotland, UK.
Tel.: (44-141) 955 18 01. Fax: (44-141) 955 18 02.
E-mail: eddy@inser.org
Contact: Eddy Adams.

### 1.4. Brief description of the action
The 'Encouraging Innovation' study was commissioned by Scottish Enterprise, the national economic development agency, to identify good practice in using multimedia to educate and train disaffected young people (16-20). The study highlights five exemplary projects in Germany, Ireland, the UK, the USA and Italy. It was completed in March 1998.


# II. Approach and content

### 2.1. Context, motivation and origin of the initiative
The study aims to tell of Scottish Enterprise's use of new technology to increase access to learning opportunities.

### 2.2. Target group
Socially excluded youth, who have fallen out of mainstream education and training, are the target study group.

### 2.3. Socio-educational approach
The study consisted of a global review of good practice in the field, and focused on inclusive approaches to educating excluded young people.

### 2.4. Scheduling and length of the action
The study was undertaken between August 1997 and March 1998.

### 2.5. Is your action/project in any way part of/supported by a national scheme or legislation that aims to combat social exclusion?
The project forms part of Scottish Enterprise's skills strategy as well as the organisation's commitment to improving access to opportunity.


# III. Partnerships and means used

### 3.1. Name, status and role of the main partner
Institute of Social and Economic Research (not-for-profit research agency).

### 3.2. Other partners
Scottish Enterprise National.

### 3.3. Monitoring and ongoing evaluation (monitoring, reporting tools)

### 3.4. External evaluation of the action

## IV. Resources

**4.1. Human resources**
Consultation (face-to-face and telephone) with over 50 organisations worldwide.

**4.2. Organisational and technical means**
Extensive use of Internet and e-mail.

**4.3. Financial data**
GBP 8 000.

## V. Innovative features

This action research project has identified five innovative initiatives that provide a learning platform for policy makers and practitioners. The study highlights themes and success criteria that can be transferred to other projects.

## VI. Comments

The study forms the initial stage in harnessing information communications technology to meet the needs of excluded youth. The study recommendations are now being implemented as part of the Scottish Enterprise learning technology strategy.

# I. Brief description of the action

### 1.1. Name of the project
Disaffected Youth Project.

### 1.2. Organisation undertaking the action
Neath Port Talbot County Borough Training Agency.

### 1.3. Address
Unit A, Milland Road Industrial Estate.
City: Neath. Country: UK.
Tel.: (44-1639) 63 64 67. Fax: (44-1639) 64 65 79.
E-mail:
Contact: Lawrence Silwyn.

### 1.4. Brief description of the action
To assist those young people between the ages of 16 and 19 to return to some form of education or training and to assist those 14 to 16-year-olds who are considered to be in danger of becoming disaffected, to not become so.

# II. Approach and content

### 2.1. Context, motivation and origin of the initiative
The number of young people dropping out was considered to be serious, and the Welsh Office therefore originated the project to endeavour to rectify the problem to some degree.

### 2.2. Target group (socially excluded youth, long-term unemployed, etc.; give ages and details of the populations concerned; their status)
Have refused to consider education, training or employment.
Are at a significant disadvantage in the labour market.
Have initially taken part in education, training or employment.

### 2.3. Socio-educational approach

### 2.4. Scheduling and length of the action
As long as it takes to have the person return — one week — six months.

### 2.5. Is your action/project in any way part of/supported by a national scheme or legislation that aims to combat social exclusion?
No.

# III. Partnerships and means used

### 3.1. Name, status and role of the main partner
West Wales TEC. Contract supplier.

### 3.2. Other partners
Recently — local education authority.

### 3.3. Monitoring and ongoing evaluation
Reports to and monitored by West Wales TEC.

### 3.4. External evaluation of the action
West Wales TEC and the Welsh Office.

# IV.     Resources

### 4.1.     Human resources used
Two members of staff — one full time, one part time.

### 4.2.     Organisational and technical means used
Computer for administration.

### 4.3.     Financial data
Estimate of the cost of the action: GBP 34 000.

# V.     Innovative features of the action
A project coordinator goes out to where young people collect, and with tact, tries to interest them in taking part.

# VI.     Comments

## I. Brief description of the action

### 1.1. Name of the project
Devon & Cornwall New Start Partnership Project.

### 1.2. Organisation undertaking the action
Devon & Cornwall Strategic Education Forum.

### 1.3. Address:
205 Creakavose Park,
St Stephen,
St Austell,
Cornwall, PL26 7ND.
UK.
Telephone and fax: (44-1726) 82 40 88.
E-mail: JohnNash1@compuserve.com
Contact: John Nash.

### 1.4. Brief description of the action
To test a strategy and framework for helping disaffected young people aged 14 to17 in four different geographical areas of Devon and Cornwall.

## II. Approach and content

### 2.1. Context, motivation and origin of the initiative
The project is one of 17 throughout England to research into and develop strategic responses to disaffected young people.

### 2.2. Target group (socially excluded youth, long-term unemployed, etc.)
The target group for this project is young people aged 14 to 17 who are disengaged, or at risk of becoming disengaged, from learning.

### 2.3. Socio-educational approach
The project aims to include all agencies that have concerns with our client group to provide a holistic approach to re-engagement.

### 2.4. Scheduling and length of the action
The action phase of the project is scheduled to start on 1 April 1998 and will completed by 31 March 1999. In reality the action may not be under way until May 1998 and may be given approval to continue to the end of April next year.

### 2.5. Is your action/project in any way part of/supported by a national scheme or legislation that aims to combat social exclusions?
Our project is one of 17 nationally which are looking at developing a national strategy to combat disaffection.

## III. Partnerships and means used

### 3.1. Name, status and role of the main partner
The main partner in the project is Prosper, formerly Devon & Cornwall Training and Enterprise Council. They are the contract holders for the project.

### 3.2. Other partners
The other main partners are Cornwall & Devon Careers Ltd., Cornwall local education authority, Cornwall youth service, Devon local education authority and Devon Youth Service.

### 3.3. Monitoring and ongoing evaluation

The Strategic Development Group, three area action groups and our local evaluators carry out the monitoring and evaluation of the project.

### 3.4. External evaluation of the action

Both a local and a national evaluator are evaluating the project. The local evaluator is looking primarily at whether we have succeeded in our objective. The national evaluators aim is to pull together good practice and ideas from the 17 projects.

## IV. Resources

### 4.1. Human resources used

The human resource within the project comprises of a project coordinator, project administrator and three project managers. However, we utilise the human resources of our partner organisations wherever possible.

### 4.2. Organisational and technical means used (facilities, new technology)

We are very reliant on our partner organisation for our facilities and technology. The project has no funding for premises and only a small budget for Information Technology etc.

### 4.3. Financial data

The overall direct cost of the project is GBP 250 000 over 18 months, from 1 October 1997 to 31 March 1999. These are for operating costs with approximately 65 % being for our human resource.

## V. Innovative features of the project

We are not aiming to 're-invent the wheel' with the action our project is taking. The innovative approach is done to the emphasis on the holistic agency approach. We wish to develop strong partnerships that can carry this work forward beyond the life of the project.

## VI. Comments

# I. Brief description of the action

**1.1. Name of the project**
Kent Behaviour Service.

**1.2. Organisation undertaking the action**
Kent County Council LEA. (Stuart Smith).

**1.3. Address**
(No address listed)
City: Country:
Tel. Fax: (44-1622) 60 57 42.
Contact: Stuart Smith.

**1.4. Brief description of the action:**
Prevention of exclusion from school.
Education of excluded pupils.
Reintegration of excluded pupils.
Identification of alternative education programmes.

# II. Approach and content

**2.1. Context, motivation and origin of the initiative**
Legal requirement to educate all pupils, even those unable to get or keep a school place.

**2.2. Target group (socially excluded youth, long-term unemployed, etc.; give ages and details of the populations concerned; their status)**
Socially excluded youth aged 6 to 10 years.
Approximately 600 per year — 1 200 at any one time.

**2.3. Socio-educational approach**
Education.
Behaviour management.
Pupil and family therapy.

**2.4. Scheduling and length of the action**

**2.5. Is your action/project in any way part of/supported by a national scheme or legislation that aims to combat social exclusion?**
GB education law relating to excluded pupils.

# III. Partnerships and means used

**3.1. Name, status and role of the main partner**

**3.2. Other partners**

**3.3. Monitoring and ongoing evaluation**

**3.4. External evaluation of the action**

## IV.    Resources

**4.1.    Human resources used**

200 teachers; five youth and community teams; educational welfare officers; five educational psychologists; young offender teams.

**4.2.    Organisational and technical means used**

**4.3.    Financial data**

Estimate of the cost of the action: GBP 5 million per annum.

## V.    Innovative features of the action

Multi-agency networks.

## VI.    Comments

## I. Brief description of the action

### 1.1. Name of the project
Training for Work.

### 1.2. Organisation undertaking the action
IBM.

### 1.3. Address
IBM Corporate Social responsibility Centre.
76 Upper Ground,
London SE1 9PZ,
UK.
Tel.: (44-171) 202 31 87.
Fax: (44-171) 261 08 16.
E-mail: celia_moore@uk.ibm.com
Contact: Celia Moore.

### 1.4. Brief description of the action
IBM is developing six projects in Europe which use technology to adapt and deliver programmes for vocational training, career choice and job matching, for disadvantaged unemployed groups. Each project is developed with training partners. The IBM projects are applying the latest developments in technology for learning to do this — distributed learning software and multimedia. For example the scheme with Brunel University, UK, will design a programme specifically to attract unqualified young black men to the learning process, and place this accessibly on their estate. Training for Asian women will be culturally adapted through the concept of home-based learning groups. Both programmes will use distributed learning software to allow self-paced flexible learning and on-line tutor support. Other projects in the European programme are developing learning software adapted to the needs of the unemployed, e.g. in France a 'portfolio of competence' that helps unqualified young people identify interests and aptitudes and eventually builds to a record of lifelong learning. In Portugal our partners are developing interactive materials for skill assessment, selection of training and job-search skills, to be made available at 'one-stop-shops'. The results from these projects will be made available throughout Europe for others to adapt to local situations. In Ireland a course based on the design of computer games is being adapted to stimulate and motivate young people who are out of school.

## II. Approach and content

### 2.1. Context, motivation and origin of the initiative
IBM's corporate social responsibility programme applies IBM technology and skills to issues of significant social and economic concern, where use of our resources can initiate and support change management.

### 2.2. Target group
The six projects target one or more of the following groups who lack relevant skills:
— young people
— long-term unemployed
— women returning to work
— people with disabilities.

### 2.3. Socio-educational approach
— Separate training facilities are providing for the target groups;
— education programmes are customised to specific needs of target group;
— individual training plans;

— use of multimedia courseware for motivation and to support the learning process;
— use of distributed learning networks to allow flexible, individual study.

**2.4. Scheduling and length of the action**
Projects start in 1998 and run for three years as pilot programmes.

**2.5. Is your action/project in any way part of/supported by a national scheme or legislation, which aims to combat social exclusion? Please describe**
Project in Portugal links with a government initiative to combat social exclusion.

## III. Partnerships and means used

**3.1. Name, status and role of the main partner**
IBM. Private company. Initiation of programme and resource provider — technology and services.

**3.2. Other partners**
— Denmark: *Naestved Kommune*, *HK Moduldata*, Royal Danish School of Education (DLH).
— France: CFA Stephenson, Paris.
— Ireland: Senior College Ballyfermot and Youthreach centres.
— Portugal: *Centro de Reabilitacao Proffissional de Gaia*.
— UK: Brunel University, Knowsley Community College.

**3.3. Monitoring and ongoing evaluation**
Monitoring and reporting will be quantitative and qualitative.

**3.4. External evaluation of the action**
An external evaluator is to be appointed.

## IV. Resources

**4.1. Human resources used (teachers, guardians)**
Teachers, facilitators, mentors.

**4.2. Organisational and technical means used**
— All projects have their own facilities — either already existing or developed specifically for the project.
— All projects are using networked computer systems.
— Five of the projects are using distributed learning software to enable flexible learning and distance education.
— Some of the projects will use groupware for collaboration between staff and learners.
— Projects will use the Internet for learning resources and for peer interaction (e.g. on-line discussion).
— One or more projects will use video conferencing.

**4.3. Financial data**
IBM's investment for technology and services will be a minimum of USD 2 million. The partners are providing teaching staff, mentors, educational content developers, facilities, complimentary technology and operating costs.

## V. Innovative features of the action
Projects will use distributed learning software with the following capabilities:
— enable training to be located at various community sites or at home;

— deliver learning materials and monitor student use;
— record student attainments against standards;
— e-mail contact with tutor;
— sharing of documents by teachers/students;
Projects will develop new interactive software programmes to assess training needs and plan learning programme, and for job placement.

**VI.      Comments**

Full details of IBM's projects are available on our website: **www.ibm.com/community/comm1.html**

# I. Brief description of the action

### 1.1. Name of the project
One Step.

### 1.2. Organisation undertaking the action
Royal Borough of Kensington and Chelsea Community Education.

### 1.3. Address
Campden Institute, 95 Lancaster Road.
City: London W11 I00. Country: England.
Tel: (44-171) 221 44 25. Fax: (44-171) 221 07 27.
E-mail: edujn@rbkc.gov.uk
Contact: Jane Ayshford.

### 1.4. Brief description of the action
Short courses and workshops for un-waged 16- to 24-year-olds in small groups in an informal supportive setting. Providing faster courses and second chance education opportunities.

# II. Approach and content

### 2.1. Context, motivation and origin of the initiative
Group of young mothers meeting — wanting to improve their labour-market skills. Funding sought for tutors (local authority youth service).

### 2.2. Target group (socially excluded youth, long-term unemployed, etc.; give ages and details of the populations concerned; their status)
Aged 16 to 24, unemployed, few or no qualifications, no work experience. Young mothers, refugees, young people with learning difficulties, homeless young people, from a wide range of ethnic, cultural and socioeconomic backgrounds.

### 2.3. Socio-educational approach
Informal approach; individual learning plans; tutor and youth worker and/or volunteer with group (6-12).
Provision of creche for under five years.

### 2.4. Scheduling and length of the action
Three 'terms' per annum. Each 10-12 weeks in length.
Enrolment is termly until the participant moves on.

### 2.5. Is your action/project in any way part of/supported by a national scheme or legislation that aims to combat social exclusion?
Links with Welfare to Work, New Deal, Gateway provisions.

# III. Partnerships and means used

### 3.1. Name, status and role of the main partner
Royal Borough of Kensington and Chelsea Community Education.

### 3.2. Other partners
(ESF received from 1990-97).

### 3.3. Monitoring and ongoing evaluation
Self-assessment.

**3.4.    External evaluation of the action**
External inspections.


## IV.    Resources

**4.1.    Human resources used**
Tutors, youth workers, creche assistants, volunteers, and administrative help.

**4.2.    Organisational and technical means used**
Network of multimedia computers, Internet.

**4.3.    Financial data**
Estimate of the cost of the action:
GBP 120 000 approximately per annum.


## V.    Innovative features of the action
— Teaching multimedia skills to those with any basic education.
— Integration of all young people within project.
— Joint staffing policy (i.e. tutor + youth worker).


## VI.    Comments

# I. Brief description of the action

### 1.1. Name of the project
Citizen Connect.

### 1.2. Organisation undertaking the action
Lifeskills International Ltd.

### 1.3. Address
Wharfebank House, Ilkley Road, Otley, LS21 3JP.
City: Otley. Country: England.
Tel.: (44-1943) 85 10 51. Fax: (44-1943) 85 12 40.
E-mail: b.robinson@citizenconnect.co.uk
Contact: Browen Robinson.

### 1.4. Brief description of the action
We are using the power of the Internet and new technology to establish an integrated development programme which will provide individuals with an on-line resource for careers information and guidance, for life skills and key skills learning, for the learning of job-seeking and job-keeping skills and the development of action plans. In the process the programme will promote self-management and enhance its skills.

# II. Approach and content

### 2.1. Context, motivation and origin of the initiative
A company with a long history of developing life skills teaching materials, with the promotion of self-managed open-learning materials, with experience of community education and development, combining its talents and resources with its specialists and local careers and guidance agencies.

### 2.2. Target group (socially excluded youth, long-term unemployed, etc.; give ages and details of the populations concerned; their status)
Initially those covered by the government's Welfare to Work/New Deal, but moving on to other groups (single parents, older unemployed) as they are drawn into the provision.

### 2.3. Socio-educational approach
The use of new technology and a long experience of designing learner-centred materials to improve development of self-esteem and confidence, which can be built on to put individuals more in charge of their lives and their futures. To be delivered through existing local agencies.

### 2.4. Scheduling and length of the action
Development happening currently. Feedback shaping the product, full delivery and access available in UK from September onwards.

### 2.5. Is your action/project in any way part of/supported by a national scheme or legislation that aims to combat social exclusion?
Development happening in consultation with government agencies, local authorities, New Deal deliverers, careers services and local providers of programmes for educationally, economically and socially excluded groups.

# III. Partnerships and means used

### 3.1. Name, status and role of the main partner
Axia Multimedia Corporation of Canada. Expertise in providing learning and mentoring through new technology.

**3.2.** **Other partners**

On-going consultation with potential user groups.

**3.3.** **Monitoring and ongoing evaluation**

Pilot-programmes being planned and arranged to influence design and content.

**3.4.** **External evaluation of the action**

Funding for evaluation under discussion.

## IV. Resources

**4.1.** **Human resources used**

Open-learning specialists, IT programmers, teachers, careers officers, business consultants, welfare to work specialists.

**4.2.** **Organisational and technical means used**

Internet application: Director-based APP connecting to Web server, DLE.-based APP on CD-ROM partition, MPEG video on CD-ROM.

**4.3.** **Financial data**

— Quarter of a million pounds to develop the programme.
— Very cost-effective delivery.

## V. Innovative features of the action

A pioneering combination of on-line guidance and learning which is capable of reducing the user/learner's dependency on 'expert helpers'. Capable of remaining available to individuals over an extended period of development in a variety of circumstances.

## VI. Comments

The content and medium of the programme offer a unique route to the provision of careers guidance and learning in a format that encourages self-management, reduces dependency, promotes its skills and remains available to the learner over an extended period. The programme offers individualised response and options, is stimulating to use, and can have national (even continental), regional and localised job information and will be easy to keep updated. At first we believe in combining these possibilities.

# I. Brief description of the action

### 1.1. Name of the project
Bristol Education On-Line (BEON).

### 1.2. Organisation undertaking the action
ICL with partners.

### 1.3 Address
Lovelace Road, Hampshire.
City: Bracknell. Country: England.
Tel: (44-1344) 477 20 01. Fax: (44-1256) 88 35 71.
E-mail: c.g.yapp@cclnet.co.uk
Contact: Chris Yapp.

### 1.4. Brief description of the action
Creation of a school network across a catchment area of South Bristol.
Some 2 000 children, 200 teachers, to pilot 'national grid for learning'.
Development of a managed service for education.


# II. Approach and content

### 2.1. Context, motivation and origin of the initiative

### 2.2. Target group (socially excluded youth, long-term unemployed, etc.; give ages and details of the populations concerned; their status)
A whole catchment area of children from 5 to 16 covering 2 000 children in 11 schools in a deprived area.

### 2.3. Socio-educational approach
A whole-school approach, training all teachers, using ICT across curriculum.
Teacher training delivered remotely.

### 2.4. Scheduling and length of the action
18 months.

### 2.5. Is your action/project in any way part of/supported by a national scheme or legislation that aims to combat social exclusion?
It was a pilot in advance of government action.


# III. Partnerships and means used

### 3.1. Name, status and role of the main partner
ICL and British Telecom, joint partners.

### 3.2. Other partners
University of Exeter, School of Education.
Various software suppliers.

### 3.3. Monitoring and ongoing evaluation
Monitored by DFEE (UK Ministry for Education and Employment), also various evaluation exercises by partners.

### 3.4. External evaluation of the action
Report available from DFEE, education departments. Superhighways Initiative.

## IV. Resources

### 4.1. Human resources used
200+ teachers in schools, teacher trainers from University of Exeter, technical expertise from ICL and BT.

### 4.2. Organisational and technical means used
510+ Pentium PCs, British Telecom's network, various servers.

### 4.3. Financial data
Estimate of the cost of the action: approximately GBP 4 million.

## V. Innovative features of the action
Linking primary schools to secondary high-density of technology managed educational service rather than technology project.

## VI. Comments
Now operational on Merseyside as MEON and in development elsewhere in the UK.

# I. Brief description of the action

### 1.1. Name of the project
Youthstart, Youthchoices.

### 1.2. Organisation undertaking the action
John Wheatley College.

### 1.3. Address
1346 Shettleston Road.
City: Glasgow. Country: Scotland.
Tel.: (44-141) 778 24 26. Fax: (44-141) 771 03 51.
E-mail: JPapamichail@jwheatley.ac.uk
Contact: Jeana Papamichail.

### 1.4. Brief description of the action
An initiative designed to offer attractive training alternatives to 'disaffected' young people who do not respond positively within mainstream schooling contexts.

# II. Approach and content

### 2.1. Context, motivation and origin of the initiative
Close liaison with guidance staff in school through school/college liaison. Programme endorsed by Glasgow City Council.

### 2.2. Target group (socially excluded youth, long-term unemployed, etc.; give ages and details of the populations concerned; their status)
Unemployed young people and school refusers circa 16 years of age, residents in areas of social and economic deprivation.

### 2.3. Socio-educational approach
Core skills and vocational training supported by on-going guidance. Parental/guardian and employer input.

### 2.4. Scheduling and length of the action
May 1998 to December 1999.

### 2.5. Is your action/project in any way part of/ supported by a national scheme or legislation that aims to combat social exclusion?
Project is supported by the Scottish Office and by the Scottish Community Education Council, both of which have social inclusion for young people as a priority within their respective agendas.

# III. Partnerships and means used

### 3.1. Name, status and role of the main partner
John Wheatley College, a further education college, will coordinate the project.

### 3.2. Other partners
Partners: local secondary schools, Steathebore Business Partnership.
Transnational partners: Italy, Greece and Spain.

### 3.3. Monitoring and ongoing evaluation
Those applied in phase 1 of the programme, i.e. 1995-97, will be modified to meet needs of new programme.

**3.4.** **External evaluation of the action**

A tender document is currently being compiled, and five companies have shown an interest.

## IV.    Resources

**4.1.** **Human resources used**

Teachers, lecturers, local development workers, local youth workers, parents, guardians and employees.

**4.2.** **Organisational and technical means used**

College and business premises and where appropriate neighbourhood venues. Project will be underpinned by the promotion of IT or other core skills.

**4.3.** **Financial data**

Estimate of the cost of the action:

Overall circa GBP 200 000.

—   55 % domestic costs, i.e. match funding

—   45 % ESF support.

## V.    Innovative features of the action

A new learning menu for young and disaffected school leavers, school refusers, poor attenders, involving collaborative support from a wide range of agencies.

## VI.    Comments

This project is a follow-on from an initial Youth Start phase but seeks to enhance this with its emphasis on a new hybrid curriculum and greater parent/guardian involvement. Group empowerment will also feature.

European Commission

**Integrating all young people into society through education and training
Volume 2 — Compendium of the projects**

Luxembourg: Office for Official Publications of the European Communities

2000 — 196 pp. — 21 x 29.7 cm

Volume II:         ISBN 92-828-7634-9
Volumes I and II: ISBN 92-828-7630-6